Chicken Soup for the Soul

for the Soul®

Devotional Stories for Women

Chicken Soup for the Soul: Devotional Stories for Women
101 Daily Devotions to Comfort, Encourage, and Inspire Women
Susan M. Heim & Karen Talcott

Published by Chicken Soup for the Soul Publishing, LLC   www.chickensoup.com

The publisher gratefully acknowledges the many publishers and individuals who
granted Chicken Soup for the Soul permission to reprint the cited material.

Front cover photo courtesy of Punchstock/BLOOMimage. Back cover photo courtesy of iStockphoto. com/ zeremski. Interior and back cover illustration courtesy of iStockphoto.com/ maxtama

Cover and Interior Design & Layout by Pneuma Books, LLC

For more info on Pneuma Books, visit www.pneumabooks.com

Distributed to the booktrade by Simon & Schuster. SAN: 200-2442

Publisher's Cataloging-in-Publication Data
(Prepared by The Donohue Group)

Chicken soup for the soul : devotional stories for women : 101 daily devotions
to comfort, encourage, and inspire women / [compiled by] Susan M. Heim [and]
Karen Talcott ; foreword by Jennifer Sands.

    p. ; cm.

    ISBN: 978-1-935096-48-1

1. Christian women--Religious life--Literary collections. 2. Christian life--Anecdotes.
3. Women--Prayers and devotions. 4. Devotional literature. I. Heim, Susan M. II.
Talcott, Karen. III. Sands, Jennifer, 1964- III. Title: Devotional stories for women

PN6071.R4 C455 2009
810.8/02/0382/3522   2009934272

PRINTED IN THE UNITED STATES OF AMERICA
on acid∞free paper
18 17 16 15 14 13 12 11 10 09   01 02 03 04 05 06 07 08 09 10

Chicken Soup for the Soul

Devotional Stories for Women

101 Daily Devotions to Comfort, Encourage, and Inspire Women

Susan M. Heim
Karen Talcott

Foreword by Jennifer Sands

CSS

Chicken Soup for the Soul Publishing, LLC
Cos Cob, CT

Contents

❶

~Faith~

❷

~Motherhood~

❸

~Life Lessons~

❹

~Illness~

❺

~God's Helpers~

❻
~Parenting~

❼
~Relationships~

8

~Loss~

9

~Service to Others~

10

~Marriage~

⑪
~Self-Esteem~

Foreword

On September 11, 2001, every aspect of my life changed forever. My husband, Jim Sands, was killed in the terrorist attack on the World Trade Center—he was working on the 103rd floor of Tower One. In one single moment, I went from being a devoted, young wife and pharmacist to a devastated and angry widow. Back then, no one could have convinced me that I would ever recover from losing the love of my life. No one could have convinced me that I would ever be functional again, or that I'd even smile again. Before 9/11, I was not a believer in Christ, my knowledge of God was very limited, and I had never owned or read a Bible. So if anyone told me back then that I would one day have a Christian writing and speaking ministry, I would've suggested that they get a CAT scan.

But in that first year after 9/11, God brought many different people into my life to help draw me close to Him. They held me up, calmed me down, and turned my anger and bitterness into peace and trust. Some of them had been there all along, like my family and closest friends. Some came into my life for a fleeting moment, then they were gone and I never saw them again. Some came into my life and have since become very dear friends. It happened just as the Bible says: *Some people planted seeds of faith, others watered them, but God was causing the growth* (my paraphrase of 1 Corinthians 3:6). About a year after 9/11, I made the decision to trust Jesus with my life and my future… it was the greatest life decision I have ever made.

I thought I had reached my suffering quota. But then came another attack from a different kind of enemy. Five years after losing my husband, I was diagnosed with breast cancer. Like that fateful morning of 9/11, I once again found myself repeating over and over, *this can't be happening... this can't be happening.* My mind was spiraling out of control and I just wanted to be held by Jim's strong arms and comforted by his familiar voice. But that impossibility was even more distressing than the news of breast cancer.

So I took a deep breath and reminded myself that, like September 11, God could have stopped this serious health crisis from happening to me. He is sovereign. He has absolute supremacy and total dominion over this universe and everything in it. Then I realized I really *was* being held by strong arms... and I *did* hear a familiar voice. They weren't Jim's and they weren't literal or audible. But they were very strong and very familiar:

"I am the LORD, the God of all mankind. Is there anything too hard for me? (Jeremiah 32:27). The eternal God is a dwelling place, and underneath are His everlasting arms (Deuteronomy 33:27). All authority has been given to Me in heaven and on earth" (Matthew 28:18).

After two surgeries and thirty-five radiation treatments, I am grateful to report that I am now cancer free, for which I thank and praise God every day. And I've learned so much since the firestorm of 9/11 and my battle with breast cancer. I've discovered that God can bring triumph from tragedy. He can bring beauty from ashes. And He can bring blessings from brokenness. I marvel at how God took the worst thing that happened to me—my husband's murder—and He used it to bring forth the best thing that could ever happen to me (or to anyone)—salvation and eternal life. Sometimes when we face our greatest loss, God will bring forth our greatest gain.

• • •

I rejoiced when I was told that Chicken Soup for the Soul would be publishing a women's Christian devotional book—applause,

applause, it's about time! *Chicken Soup for the Soul* books have touched the hearts of countless readers by telling real stories from real people going through real life… what a blessing for my sisters in Christ to finally have their own *Chicken Soup for the Soul* devotional. I enjoyed the manuscript so much that I wanted to toss in a couple of my own stories, so now you have two bonus blessings at the end of the book.

So much to learn, so much to share. *Chicken Soup for the Soul: Devotional Stories for Women* is a treasure chest of vignettes from women who have learned about God's faithfulness and want to share their riches with the world. As I read their words, I feel like I'm sitting down with an old friend and a cup of tea, chatting about God's latest display of grace. This book is a botanical garden of stories that will plant seeds, water the roots, and cultivate the soil of our own heart… all while God is causing the spiritual growth. Books like this—along with the Bible—gave me the encouragement and hope I desperately needed after 9/11. And I still need encouragement and hope every day… don't we all, ladies? Life is a journey through mountains and valleys, and they come in all shapes and sizes. Reading about the experiences of other women in this very special *Chicken Soup for the Soul* book truly warms my heart, lifts my spirit, puts a smile on my face and deepens my trust in the Lord.

I can't tell you how many times after September 11 I asked, "Why? Why? Why?" And perhaps you're crawling through a valley right now and you're asking that same question. I can tell you from personal experience that God allows suffering in our lives because there is work to be done inside of us that cannot be accomplished any other way. But He also uses our trials to equip us, so that we can support other people who are going through similar circumstances. We can be an example of trusting the Lord through the adversity in our lives. We can say to them, "I was tried and tested the same way—look at what God did in my life." None of us were made to stand alone! God uses us to hold each other up and bear each other's burdens. That is the very essence of 2 Corinthians 1:3-4, and that is the very essence of this book:

Praise be to the God and Father of our Lord Jesus Christ, the Father of compassion and the God of all comfort, who comforts us in all our troubles, so that we can comfort those in any trouble with the comfort we ourselves have received from God.

I pray that *Chicken Soup for the Soul: Devotional Stories for Women* will bring you as much comfort as it brings to me. Along with peace. Healing. Guidance. Strength. Wisdom. A few giggles. And lots of inspiration. So make yourself a cup of tea, snuggle up in your favorite chair, and get ready for a book full of blessings and girlfriends and Scripture and smiles.

~Jennifer Sands
Christian Speaker and Author of
A Tempered Faith, A Teachable Faith, and *A Treasured Faith*

Introduction

*J*esus certainly knew what he was talking about when he said, "In this world you will have trouble" (John 16:33). Trials are a part of life! Some trials are small, like when your child gets permanent marker all over her new dress or you get a flat tire. Other troubles, like a cancer diagnosis or a job loss, can be catastrophic. Fortunately, Jesus reassures us in that same passage, "But take heart! I have overcome the world." He is with us through it all. And not only did Jesus give us the gift of himself, but he gave us another source of hope and inspiration: each other. Woman-to-woman, through the grace of our Father, we can overcome the challenges that come our way.

Women have always shared life's experiences with one another. In pioneer days, women would gather to quilt and sew, swapping advice and offering comfort. In the Bible, Naomi and Ruth shared their sorrows and joys, and Ruth came to know God through Naomi's counsel and friendship. Proverbs 31 says that a woman "of noble character... speaks with wisdom, and faithful instruction is on her tongue." Women were created to be there for each other, and we continue to fulfill that mission in today's world. We meet in mothers' groups, girls' night out events, book clubs, professional organizations and Christian women's circles. Women intuitively know that they can expand and enrich their lives just by gathering, talking, and listening together.

This book, *Chicken Soup for the Soul: Devotional Stories for Women*, is filled with women's personal stories and lessons learned. A woman's faith is tested—and restored—when she receives news of a breast cancer diagnosis. After her daughter dies, a mother turns to God for the strength to go on. Other women learn that by serving others, they feel God's presence most poignantly. Stories like these are life lessons that show how God heals our wounds, soothes our souls, and answers our prayers. He is an ever-present source of comfort and love. We are reminded of this in the beloved Psalm 23:1-3: "The LORD is my shepherd, I shall not be in want. He makes me lie down in green pastures, He leads me beside quiet waters, He restores my soul."

There are several ways in which you can read *Chicken Soup for the Soul: Devotional Stories for Women:*

- Start at the beginning! Spend a little time with God each day by starting at the beginning of the book and reading a page each day for inspiration.

- Pray for guidance. Holding the book closed, pray for God to guide you to just the right devotional that you need to read that day. Randomly open the book and see where the Spirit leads!

- Select a topic. If you're dealing with a particular problem, such as marital difficulties or a medical condition, turn to the appropriate chapter and select a devotional that applies to your situation.

We know that the words of wisdom from the women in this book will warm your heart and show you that God is your partner in this walk of life. Whether the path is smooth or filled with potholes, God walks with you. He might be shoulder-to-shoulder or even carrying you down the road, but He is always there.

~Susan and Karen

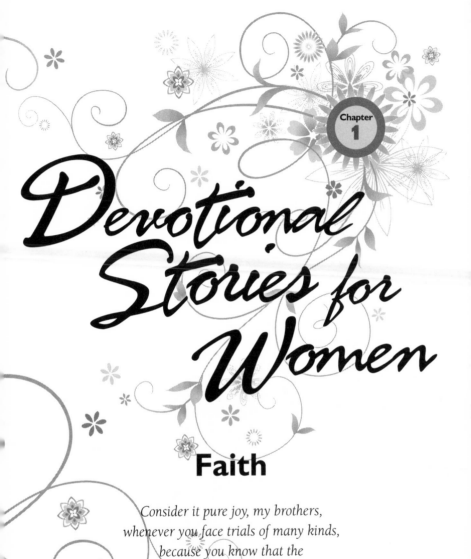

Chapter 1

Devotional Stories for Women

Faith

Consider it pure joy, my brothers,
whenever you face trials of many kinds,
because you know that the
testing of your faith develops perseverance.

~James 1:2-3

A Cool Breeze, and a Change of Heart

By Karen Talcott

I will praise you, O LORD, with all my heart;
before the "gods" I will sing your praise.
~Psalm 138:1

iving in Florida, the summer heat wears on you after awhile. The mornings start in the nineties with high humidity, and the days end in the eighties with high humidity. I often feel that our seasons are reversed from the rest of the country. About May, we tightly close up our houses and put on the air conditioner. Then we live inside for most of the summer heat. Around the end of October, the beginnings of a few cool fronts make it down to our state.

So, our expectations were high when we learned that the weatherman had forecast the first blast of cool air coming our way one night. How excited my husband and I were to open the windows in anticipation of the fresh air. That night, I awoke to the fresh breeze flowing around me. It felt so lovely to be snuggled up and yet have that hint of cold around me.

The next morning, my whole family felt alive. We were playful at breakfast while the dogs bounced around at our feet. We dug out our "cool weather clothes" for the first time in months. It was funny to laugh at how our favorite clothes had shrunk. Had my son's legs really grown that long over the summer?

With the kids off to school, I headed out for my morning walk with the dogs. The cool weather made me walk faster, and I felt so invigorated. I listened to the birds calling in the trees, watched the busy squirrels, and admired the beautiful flowers. These had all been the same sights the day before, but today my eyes were fresh. My heart filled with gratitude for the beloved garden that God created.

I think it is important to savor those moments when you really feel alive. What makes you wake up and start the day in anticipation? It could be as simple as a day of cool weather. Regardless, it is God's way of catching our attention and honoring this truly magnificent world He created.

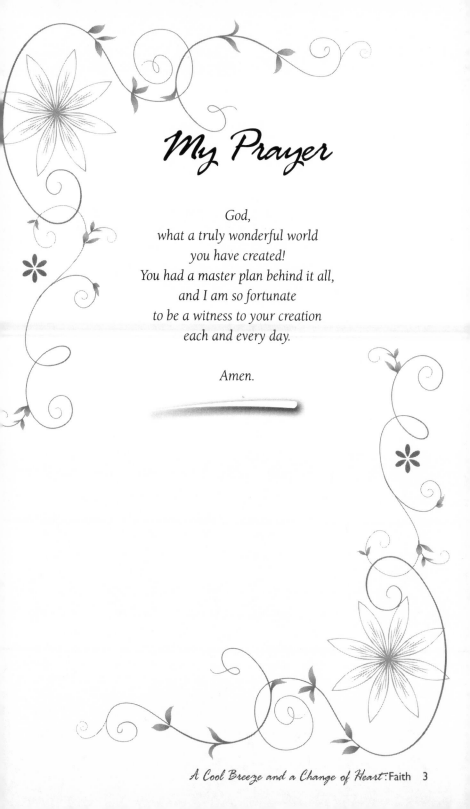

My Prayer

God,
what a truly wonderful world
you have created!
You had a master plan behind it all,
and I am so fortunate
to be a witness to your creation
each and every day.

Amen.

From Fruit of the Loom to a Car

By Robin Smith

God sets the lonely in families... You gave abundant showers, O God; you refreshed your weary inheritance. Your people settled in it, and from your bounty, O God, you provided for the poor.
~Psalm 68:6a, 9-10

When my husband and I decided to start a family, we budgeted, planned, and scheduled. Moving from a dual-income family to a single-income family was a major adjustment, but we felt it was worth the sacrifice for me to be home. We were not sure how we could make it work, but we were ready to try and felt in control.

Eight months after our daughter was born, while we were still adjusting to the changes that had occurred, God brought two precious boys, ages five and six, into our lives. The boys came with nothing, but we felt called by God to have them in our family. We adopted them, not knowing how we could provide for a family of five on one income. We had an old car that needed replacing, quite a few bills, and no extra cash, but a lot of love.

We were in awe as God provided, meeting needs as they became apparent—and often before they were even apparent. God used so many people to bless us. Our Sunday school class and my husband's employer held showers to welcome the boys to our family. Our one attempt at buying new things for them resulted in the purchases being rung up at no cost, including their Fruit of the Loom underwear! Regularly, we would find anonymously sent cards of encouragement with cash gifts.

A church family even gave us a car, and over the years as the used cars have died, we have been given two more from completely different families. One year, each student in my husband's fifth-grade class brought a gift for someone in our family and filled the space under our Christmas tree.

Our leap of faith has been a blessing as we watch God provide and direct our lives. We have since added another beautiful daughter to our family. We still attempt to plan, and things frequently do not go as expected, but God has provided abundantly and continues to provide. Clearly, He is in complete control.

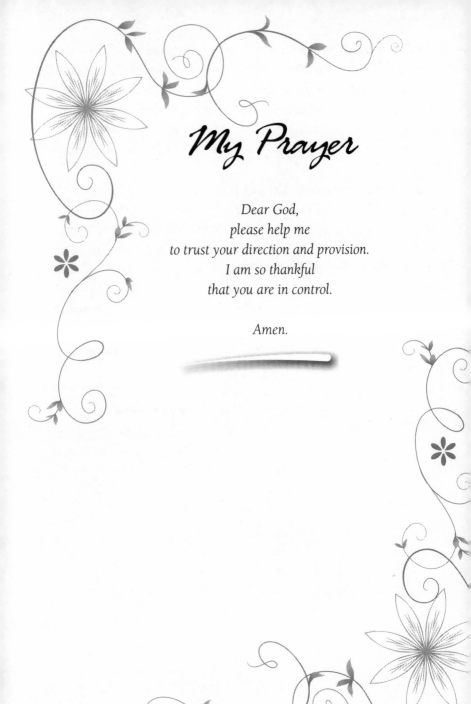

My Prayer

Dear God,
please help me
to trust your direction and provision.
I am so thankful
that you are in control.

Amen.

3

A Blessing in Disguise

By Lorie Bibbee

So do not fear, for I am with you; do not be dismayed,
for I am your God.
I will strengthen you and help you;
I will uphold you with my righteous right hand.
~Isaiah 41:10

W e were just leaving the movie theater when, out of the blue, I turned to my roommate and said, "I'm not going to have a job tomorrow."

She freaked out. "Why?! Don't say that!" she said.

I told her, "God just popped 'fear not, nor be dismayed, be strong and of good courage' in my head, and told me I wouldn't have a job after tomorrow."

She looked at me as if I'd lost my mind and said, "You're weird." Then we went home.

Strangely, there was nothing wrong at work. I had just been gone for a week traveling for my job, and I hadn't even been back to the office yet. But everything had been fine when I was last there. However, I'd known for a while it was time to move on. I just didn't have the courage to leave. I even talked to God about it in prayer and asked Him to either give me the courage or make it happen.

The next day, I went into the office just like normal. I wrote on a card the verse God had given me outside the movie theater and put it up on my office wall. Everything was fine until 5:00 P.M. My boss called a meeting. He said that times were hard, and he would be laying off some people and decreasing the salary of others.

We went into our offices, and he went around to let each person know what their fate would be. When he came into my office, I smiled and said, "I know! God told me yesterday, and I told my roommate! See, here's the verse!"

He was shocked and said, "But I didn't even think about it until today!"

The next three months were an exhilarating time of change for me. The entire direction of my life changed in ways I couldn't even hope for while I was still at my previous job. That loss turned into one of the biggest blessings in my life.

My Prayer

God, you are so good!
Thank you for preparing and providing.
You really do make a way
when there seems to be no way,
and bring hope when all hope seems gone.
Lord, thank you for giving me courage,
and I pray for anyone
who is facing major change now.
Please let them see your hand clearly.

Amen.

4

Chicken Soup for the Soul

Against All Odds

By Lisa Murphy

For I know the plans I have for you, declares the Lord,
plans to prosper you and not to harm you,
plans to give you hope and a future.
~Jeremiah 29:11

met a woman whose whole life had been about worldly pleasures. It was all about how she looked and feeling good. She was
a beautiful, sweet woman, but her lifestyle led her to drugs and
alcohol. Eventually, she ended up penniless and homeless.

Against all odds, God brought her to rehab. As she saw the
changes that God was making in her life, she became determined to
focus on Him. However, her friends were turning away, and she lost
her job. I told her I felt that God was clearing a path for her and asked
her what was on her heart. She said she felt led to be a missionary.

We called a mission school, and she cried tears of joy when she
hung up the phone. God was calling her there. Although she would
need thousands of dollars and a plane ticket to begin in two weeks,
we both had faith that God would provide.

We sent letters to her remaining friends and asked for any
financial support to be sent directly to the school. As the deadline

approached, it seemed that God was, in fact, providing the tuition. The last hurdle was the plane ticket.

I announced at a Bible study what my friend was doing. At the end, a fellow mom handed me a check for $100. I called my friend and told her I thought we could get her a one-way ticket. But when we started checking air fares, the cheapest flight to her destination was $444.

We stopped and prayed, "Father, we know you want her at this school. Please make it simple. In Jesus' name, Amen."

I turned to look at the computer, but the screen looked blurry. I told my friend that I could not read the computer. At that moment, her cell phone rang.

She screamed, "It is my pilot friend that I haven't spoken to in months!"

She told the pilot that she had to get to Texas by Sunday.

He said, "I will take care of everything. You will be there by Sunday, and it will cost you $100 or less."

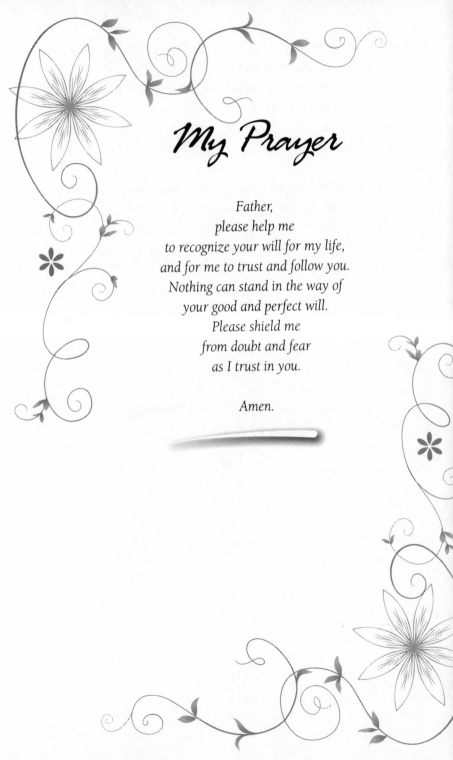

My Prayer

Father,
please help me
to recognize your will for my life,
and for me to trust and follow you.
Nothing can stand in the way of
your good and perfect will.
Please shield me
from doubt and fear
as I trust in you.

Amen.

In God We Trust

By Francinne Cascio Lawrence

He who trusts in himself is a fool,
but he who walks in wisdom is kept safe.
~Proverbs 28:26

With my family and friends living on the other side of the country, my first pregnancy was a pretty lonely, scary experience. I tended to worry about most things anyway, but concern for the health of my developing baby seemed to grip me with a fierce, relentless fear.

I was working as a chaplain at the time in a hospital just outside of Washington, D.C. It was a setting filled with the sights, sounds, and smells of distressing situations. But, looking back, I realize my large, egg-shaped belly—which my precious unborn perpetrated with energetic kicks like a baby chick making its way from its shell—brought forth stories and unlocked emotions within my patients that would have otherwise remained tucked away.

One afternoon, while on a break, I crossed the street in front of the hospital and entered a lovely park filled with trees and grasses, and all the smells of the energy and vivacity of life. I walked around and around its perimeter with my head down, as if pacing, but in a circular motion.

The question, "How can I know my baby is all right?" kept pace with my steps as it repeated itself in my mind. In my heart of hearts, I searched desperately for my answer as I eyed each passing blade of grass and crackled each tentative twig under my feet.

As unannounced as a fleeting thought, my answer appeared. It lay on the earthen floor at the toe of my last footfall—an ordinary penny looking up at me as if planted there with purpose and intention. I probably would have simply walked over it without ever noticing except that, in that moment, the inscription on the coin appeared larger than life and was easily read, even though my eyes were five feet from the ground.

"In God We Trust" rose up to me like a prophetic revelation. Not through logic, reason, or rational justification did I find inner peace that afternoon. Rather, my solace came from the jolting reality of a basic truth inscribed on the simplest of coins.

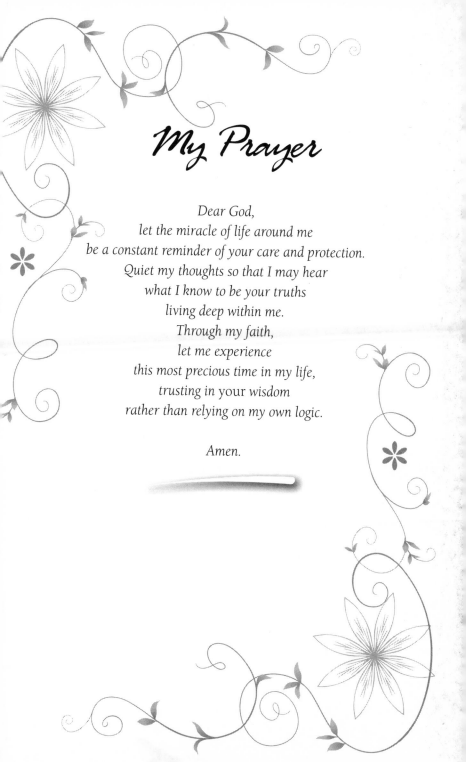

My Prayer

Dear God,
let the miracle of life around me
be a constant reminder of your care and protection.
Quiet my thoughts so that I may hear
what I know to be your truths
living deep within me.
Through my faith,
let me experience
this most precious time in my life,
trusting in your wisdom
rather than relying on my own logic.

Amen.

6

A Woman of Faith

By Phyllis Saxton

I lift up my eyes to the hills—
where does my help come from?
My help comes from the LORD,
the Maker of heaven and earth.
~Psalm 121:1-2

My mother, Sarah Elizabeth (called Sallie), was born in 1889 on a ranch in northern Colorado at the foot of the Rocky Mountains. Her love of the high country sustained her throughout her life. Daily, she was taught the high living standards of that time by her parents, when hard work was necessary and obedience absolute.

Our large family was raised in the same manner, although when I was born, we lived in town. My mother insisted that we follow the Golden Rule, and honesty was paramount. Rules were taught with love and kindness, and by example. While she was private about her feelings, Sallie lived them every day. And she loved America.

Any time the flag was on display or the National Anthem was played, we were to stand at attention and hold our hand over our hearts. We were teased a lot for these actions by our friends, but we always did as Mom said. My younger brother and I memorized "Stars and Stripes Forever" and sang it often when requested. Our duet could no doubt be repeated today.

The World War II years were difficult for my mother. Three of her sons went overseas, and my sister's husband was also serving. Later, another brother of mine was in the Korean "conflict." Our family depended on Sallie's prayers and courage. Fortunately, everyone came home safely.

Mother's divorce and relocation to Idaho were handled with the same steely resolve. Not many women left a marriage in that day, and this step was frowned upon, but she felt it was the only way. Many trials and tribulations never caused my mother's faith in God to waver.

I am so grateful to have had Sallie for my mother and to have her genuine faith passed on to me. My life has been richer for it. Whenever I have a doubt, I stop and say, "What would Mom do?" Right away, I have my answer.

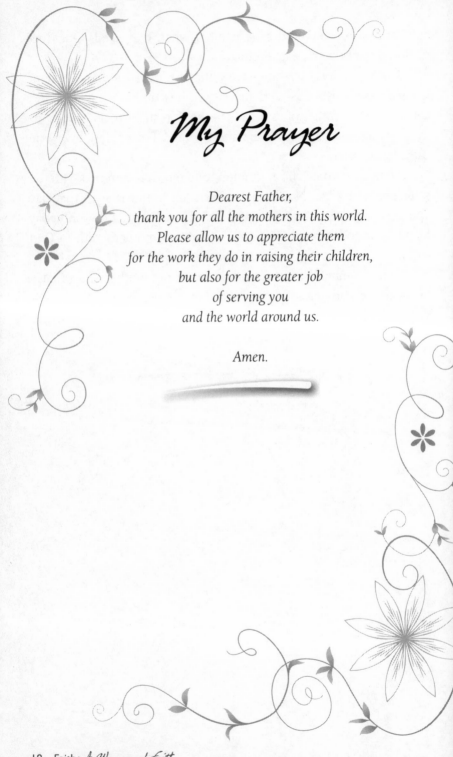

My Prayer

Dearest Father,
thank you for all the mothers in this world.
Please allow us to appreciate them
for the work they do in raising their children,
but also for the greater job
of serving you
and the world around us.

Amen.

7

The Trees Needed to Be Cut

By Karen Talcott

Ask and it will be given to you;
seek and you will find; know and the door will be opened to you.
~Matthew 7:7

It was hurricane season again in Florida and time for the palm trees to be cut. We were always warned before hurricane season to prepare and cut back the palm fronds and coconuts. They could become missiles during a hurricane, doing great damage to the windows in the house.

One morning as I left the house, I decided to ask God for help in finding a tree cutter. I quickly said a short prayer asking God to send someone to my house who could cut the trees back while offering to perform the work for a reasonable cost. I then went about my day without giving it a second thought. I knew that once my prayer had been asked, I needed to have faith that God would help me out.

That night as I played in the front yard with my kids, a little red pick-up truck entered the neighborhood. The driver drove around for a while before coming back to stop directly in front of my house. He stopped to make small talk and admire my collie.

For some reason, I asked if he cut trees and, sure enough, he did—and he had time to take care of them that night! Of course, the price was going to be a deciding factor in the whole deal, but the price he quoted was the exact number in my head.

I asked for his business card when he was done. It read: *Respectful Tree Service, Doing God's Work for 15 Years*. A jolt ran through my body as I read the words. I did not need any more proof that God had helped me that day.

My Prayer

God,
thank you for allowing us
to send short quick prayers up to you in Heaven.
You always hear our needs,
be they big or small,
and then respond
in your most loving way.

Amen.

"I knew you'd do a great job! You came with the highest recommendation!"

Come Closer

By Olivia Bibbee, age 12

But you, O LORD, have mercy on me;
raise me up, that I may repay them.
I know that you are pleased with me,
for my enemy does not triumph over me.
In my integrity you uphold me
and set me in your presence forever.
~Psalm 41:10-12

All during my sixth-grade year, I was tormented by a group of classmates. At recess, they would tell me to go away, and then whisper excitedly to each other upon my exit. At first, it was a simple "We need to talk in private for a moment." That turned into "Oh, I have an itch. You go ahead. We'll catch up later." That ended up as a "Could you just go away?" The remarks got less innocent and more hurtful as the year grew old.

During the first couple of weeks, I thought I had a best friend. I had met her in volleyball camp over the summer, and we were psyched to be in the same class. It started as tons of secret slumber parties and whispering at recess. Then she got other friends and left me hanging. Now she was one of the girls who told me to go away, and it hurt even more when she said it.

Every day, I would come home crying and crying. I tried to put my emotions away in my schoolwork. Then I tried dance. Then I just gave up. I never once tried giving my emotions to God... the only one who was capable of taking them.

Now that I'm a little bit older, I am ashamed at how I behaved. When I was thrown away by my classmates, it was just God's way of saying, "Come closer." Instead of crying in the bathroom, I should have been on my knees praying. (Well, maybe not on my knees... I *was* in the bathroom!)

I now know that life's difficulties are God's way of saying, "You are off track and have gone astray. Come closer to me, and I will love you to the fullest."

I started praying and, what do you know, it worked! I didn't gain any new friends at first—it was the end of the year by the time I came to my senses—but I did gain faith in God. I built a very strong relationship with Him that lasts to this very day. And who knows? Maybe next year I will have a friend who will last forever. At least I know now that God will always be my friend.

My Prayer

Dear Lord,
help me to understand
the troubles and triumphs you put before me.
Remind me to throw down my sorrows unto you...
because you are the only one
capable of catching them.
Lead me back to you when I have gone astray.
Draw me closer to your love
and take me under your wing.

Amen.

Trusting in the flow of Life

By Christy Holstead Semple

Blessed are those who trust in the Lord
and have made the Lord their hope and confidence.
They are like trees planted along a riverbank,
with roots that reach deep into the water.
Such trees are not bothered by the heat
or worried by long months of drought.
Their leaves stay green,
and they go right on producing delicious fruit.
~Jeremiah 17:7-8

I wanted to have a baby. For five years, my husband and I had been hoping for this blessing to come into our lives, but it had not come to pass. I said many prayers during those years, each one more urgent and hopeful than the last. My anxiety turned to a more intense worry as the months and then years passed.

The doctors and specialists we visited did not use encouraging words with us; rather, we heard words like "never" and "impossible." Doubt began to fill my mind, and it seeped into my prayers. I started to wonder why my prayers weren't working. My faith was challenged as I began to question my beliefs.

One day, I was reading Jeremiah, and the verse 17:7-8 really spoke to me. I realized I had not been trusting in God. I had been putting my trust in my own hope and willpower instead.

I looked out at the beautiful trees God had created and thought about the message of trust they represented. With a new awareness, I noticed their calm nature, and I thought of their roots deep in the ground, like the deep roots of faith. It was then that I moved forward in a new way. And then, wonderful things began to happen.

My husband and I met a doctor who was positive and encouraging. We were filled with the confident expectation of becoming parents. A few months later, we rejoiced at learning the news that we were going to have a baby.

Trusting in the ever-present flow of life and putting confidence in God rather than my own determination have brought this gift of love into my life and opened more pathways to greater and greater good than ever before.

My Prayer

Heavenly Father,
help me to always see
the true flow of life
that is ever-present in
and through me every moment of every day.
Regardless of appearances of limitation to this flow,
help me to trust that it is always there,
producing beautiful expressions
of love and creativity.

Amen.

A Fool and His Gold

By Nancy Purcell

Of what use is money in the hand of a fool,
since he has no desire to get wisdom?
~Proverbs 17:15

Growing up, I lived in an apartment two blocks from the railroad tracks. My mother worked two jobs, and my six-year-old sister was my babysitter; she was in first grade, and I was in kindergarten. When my mother remarried, we moved to a real house in the country. Life was better, food was in greater supply, and our house soon filled with lovely things.

I married at nineteen and raised three children. Later, I found the courage to divorce my husband, who was a gambler and unfaithful. With all of my children gone, I learned to live alone and depend on myself. But through all the ups and downs in my life, my faith remained strong. I knew God was always by my side.

Many years later, I married again. This wonderful man came from a family with considerable wealth, and although I continued to work, my lifestyle had moved up a notch.

Ten years later, my father-in-law died, leaving behind his wife of sixty-two years of marriage—a woman who had never paid a bill and lived without a belief system to carry her through the future. She questions me about my faith.

"How do you know there's a heaven?"

"If there is a God, why didn't He answer my prayers and save my husband?"

I answer her questions with words that come through me from an inner Spirit: I believe because He told us so.

It is sad to see someone you love refuse God's invitation. He knocks, but she will not or cannot open the door. She finds herself alone and afraid at age ninety-two, when all she needs to do is answer the door and let Him in.

My Prayer

Dear God,
my rock and my salvation,
help me to be ever mindful of what is important.
When I am generous to others,
let it be because I am grateful for
the peace your love has granted me.
You cannot purchase a ticket to heaven.
Entry is free to all who believe in you.

Amen.

The Saturday Morning Miracle

By Cynthia J. Freels

"Therefore I tell you, do not worry about your life,
what you will eat or drink...
Look at the birds of the air;
they do not sow or reap or store away in barns,
and yet your heavenly Father feeds them.
Are you not much more valuable than they?
Who of you by worrying can add a single hour to his life?"
~Matthew 6:25-27

My husband was the director and I was the volunteer coordinator for a homeless shelter in South Florida. There were eleven small apartment units, and one adult member of each family could shop for free on Saturday mornings from a small pantry on the property. The food was collected from churches, schools and other organizations throughout our community.

A couple of weeks before Palm Sunday, it was brought to our attention that we were running out of food and would need to have a food drive. Well, it takes a couple of weeks to organize a drive, so alternative plans had to be made.

The first week during the shortage, we went to the local food bank and were able to get enough for that weekend. But the second week was a different story. I had been praying all week, and I awoke on Saturday morning, worrying.

"Dear God, what are we going to do today? There is no food for our families."

When I arrived at the property that morning, I sat in the car for a minute and sent up one more prayer to Our Heavenly Father. Then I got out of the car and began to walk in. With a sigh, I put my key in the lock, unlocked the door and looked inside. I couldn't believe the sight that met my eyes. Bags and boxes of food were all over the floor.

I started to laugh and giggle, praising God and thanking Him for all his gifts. Why had I worried so much? I learned later that a Christian school had delivered on Friday all these bags and boxes of food that the schoolchildren had been collecting. What a wonderful gift for our homeless families!

My husband and I have since retired, but the homeless shelter remains active. God continues to call my husband and me in many ways, and we continue to hear and obey. The jobs are not as big, but they are just as important. And, best of all, I do not worry as much!

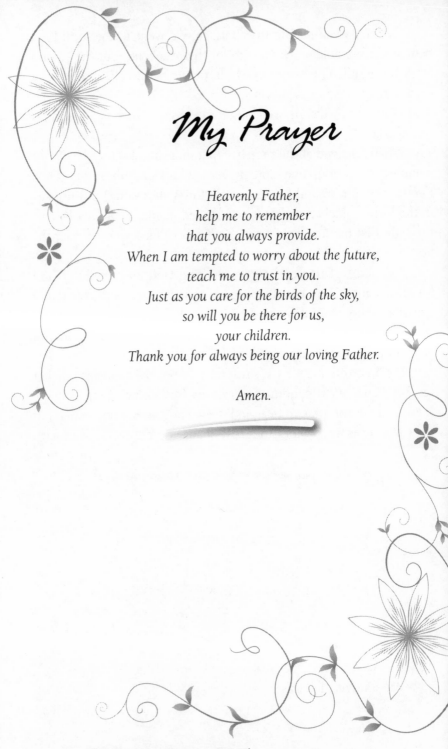

My Prayer

Heavenly Father,
help me to remember
that you always provide.
When I am tempted to worry about the future,
teach me to trust in you.
Just as you care for the birds of the sky,
so will you be there for us,
your children.
Thank you for always being our loving Father.

Amen.

Running from God

By Lorie Bibbee

But in your hearts set apart Christ as Lord.
Always be prepared to give an answer to everyone
who asks you to give the reason for the hope that you have.
But do this with gentleness and respect.
~1 Peter 3:15

I was holding my youngest child, waving as my husband took our older kids off to school, when my new next-door neighbor drove up in her brand-new convertible. She and her little one were headed to the beach, and she asked if we would join them. To be neighborly (and because I love driving in convertibles!), I said yes.

Our little guys became new friends as they splashed in the waves and dug holes in the sand, while I started talking with my new neighbor. A few minutes later, another woman joined us, and her son started playing with our boys. She said that she and her boyfriend, her son's father, had just gotten in a car and driven here to Florida from somewhere cold. They drove straight to the beach, climbed out of the car, and decided to stay.

"Wow," my neighbor said. "What brought on that kind of road trip?"

She replied, "My boyfriend's mom is a Christian, and she keeps trying to tell us to get married and find God. We just decided to run away from her and her God."

I couldn't help myself. I started bubbling over with laughter, and then I reached right out and hugged her.

"You might be running from God," I told her, "but He got here ahead of you! I'm a Christian, too, and I'm here to tell you that He loves you. There is no place you can run and hide!"

We talked for quite a while. She felt safe asking questions of a stranger, things she was uncomfortable about asking her mother-in-law. By the time we left, we had prayed together, and she had a new respect for her soon-to-be mother-in-law.

My new neighbor was a little freaked out, but that's okay. Her old next-door neighbor became "Jesus" at The Holy Land Experience in Orlando. It seems she can't run and hide from God either. He's got big plans for my new neighbor someday!

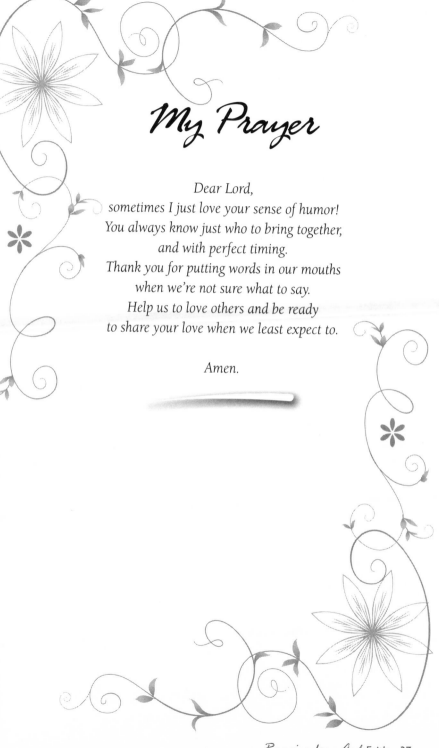

My Prayer

Dear Lord,
sometimes I just love your sense of humor!
You always know just who to bring together,
and with perfect timing.
Thank you for putting words in our mouths
when we're not sure what to say.
Help us to love others and be ready
to share your love when we least expect to.

Amen.

Devotional Stories for Women

Motherhood

*But we were gentle among you,
like a mother caring for her little children.*

~1 Thessalonians 2:7

13

Baby's Breath

By Susan M. Heim

*The LORD God formed the man from the dust of the ground
and breathed into his nostrils the breath of life,
and the man became a living being.*
~Genesis 2:7

Nineteen years ago, I was a new mother. I'd always wanted to have a child, but, like most new parents, I was somewhat surprised at how overwhelming it was to keep my baby happy twenty-four hours a day.

One particular evening, my little son had been overly fussy, and both of us were worn out from his crying. Finally, exhausted, I lay down on the couch with the baby stretched across my chest. Both baby and I fell fast asleep.

A while later, I awoke to the bright glow of the moon shining through the window. I opened my eyes to find this tiny body still sprawled across me, his little hands tightly clenching the sides of my shirt. His bow-shaped mouth was slightly open, and his sweet baby breath caressed my face with each rise and fall of his chest. His skin was translucent, and his dear face was the picture of innocence bathed in the moonlight.

Tears came to my eyes as I realized that this delicate child, nestled close, had truly stolen my heart. I felt wondrously blessed to have this precious son.

From that moment on, whenever I grew frustrated with my attempts to keep my child satisfied—and, believe me, over the next nineteen years, there were many of those times—I'd transport myself back to that perfect night, to feel again the soft weight of his warm body on mine and his light breath blowing across my face.

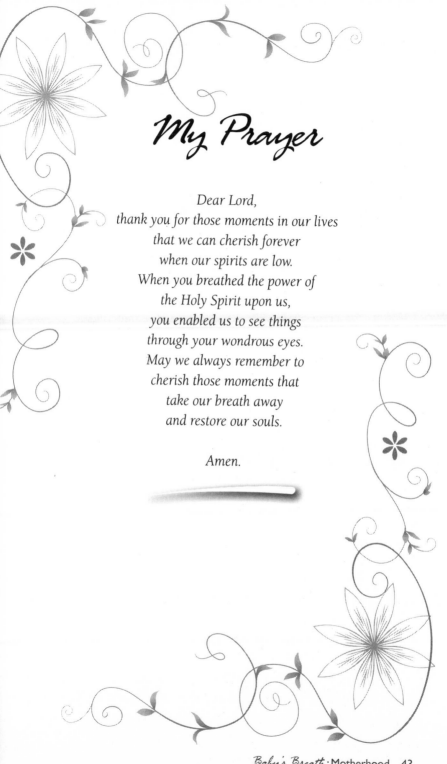

My Prayer

Dear Lord,
thank you for those moments in our lives
that we can cherish forever
when our spirits are low.
When you breathed the power of
the Holy Spirit upon us,
you enabled us to see things
through your wondrous eyes.
May we always remember to
cherish those moments that
take our breath away
and restore our souls.

Amen.

14

Love and Potato Chips

By Maria Rodgers O'Rourke

God said, "This is the sign of the covenant that I make
between me and you and every living creature that is with you,
for all future generations:
I have set my bow in the clouds
and it shall be a sign of the covenant between me and the earth."
~Genesis 8:12-13

One night at the dinner table, our eight-year-old daughter was stalling, refusing to eat her corn. Our rule is that if you don't eat your whole dinner, including the vegetable, you don't get any dessert or snacks later. On this particular night, she felt so strongly about not eating her corn that she still left the vegetable on her plate, even when she was reminded of the rule.

As my daughter moved toward the family room, she spied a nearly empty bag of chips on the counter. She picked up the bag and put some in her mouth. I raised a finger and said, "Uh-uh [no]!" Immediately, she dashed to the trash can, opened her mouth, and pushed the chips into the can.

I was stunned! What a precious thing to do! I instantly scooped her into my arms and thanked her for her honesty. My hug caught her off guard; she pulled back at first, fearful of a reprimand. Instead,

I kissed her and told her how proud I was of her. My heart was filled with overflowing love for this child who just a few minutes prior had been testing my patience to its limit.

A covenant is distinct from a contract in that a contract is based on living up to stated expectations while a covenant is based on relationship and love. If either of us fails in our duty, the contract is broken. As shown in his rainbow, God invites us into a covenant relationship with Him.

We are so blessed that God loves with covenant love. He helps moms to love first and enforce the rules later. When the rules are broken, both continue to love. The constant is love, no matter what.

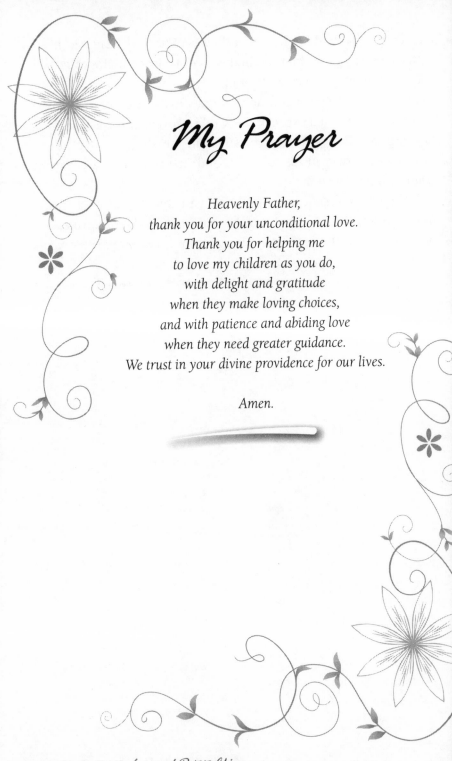

My Prayer

Heavenly Father,
thank you for your unconditional love.
Thank you for helping me
to love my children as you do,
with delight and gratitude
when they make loving choices,
and with patience and abiding love
when they need greater guidance.
We trust in your divine providence for our lives.

Amen.

15

My Treasure from God

By Clara Riveros

But He knows the ways that I take;
when He has tested me, I will come forth as gold.
~Job 23:10

was thirty-seven years old when I learned I was expecting my third child. With two older children and working a full-time job, it was difficult to accept this pregnancy.

Because of my age, I scheduled an amniocentesis to check for abnormalities. My doctor agreed but changed his mind just before the test because I had two healthy daughters. I now feel strongly that God was protecting my baby. As I wasn't crazy about being pregnant, I might have considered termination if the test had revealed a birth defect.

Just one hour after delivering my daughter, Melissa, the doctor told my husband and me that our daughter was a "Mongoloid," or mentally retarded. This brought the most agonizing pain my heart had ever gone through. I kept hoping the doctors had misdiagnosed my daughter.

The next day, a social worker showed me brochures of a home

for "these kind of children." I told her there was no way I would consider it and demanded she leave my room immediately.

We brought Melissa home, and thus began the lowest times of my life. Her health was not the best, resulting in continuous ER and doctors' visits. I struggled spiritually at first, and just couldn't accept that this was happening to me.

But even though the road was painful, my relationship with the Lord gradually renewed and strengthened. I began to realize that having Melissa, just exactly the way she is, was a gift from God. Her Down's syndrome was not a burden, but a blessing!

Today, Melissa is an adult and the apple of my eye, loved by her entire family. She is happy and in excellent health. She lives a full and productive life, and even has a part-time job at a grocery store. Her room is covered in medals she has won through Special Olympics.

Melissa has accepted Christ into her heart, and knows of Christ's perfect, free gift of forgiveness and eternal love. Many mornings she wakes up and tells me Jesus spoke to her in her dreams. It was a hard road in the beginning, but now Melissa is a treasure from God and my constant companion.

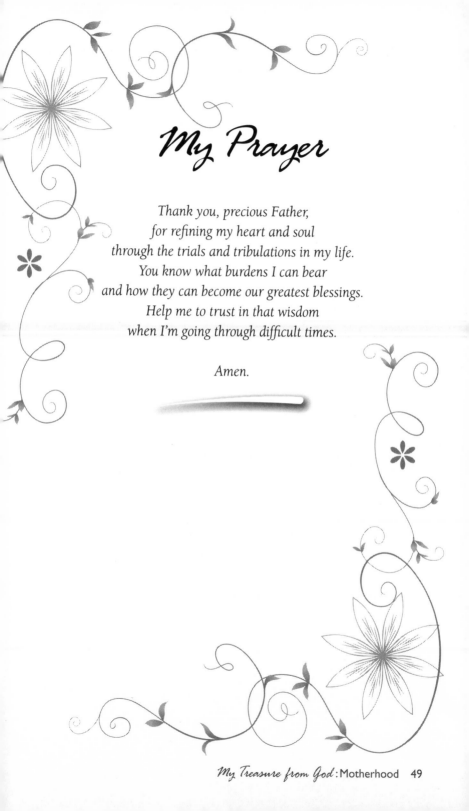

My Prayer

Thank you, precious Father,
for refining my heart and soul
through the trials and tribulations in my life.
You know what burdens I can bear
and how they can become our greatest blessings.
Help me to trust in that wisdom
when I'm going through difficult times.

Amen.

Like a Child

By Deborah L. Kaufman

And he said: I tell you the truth,
unless you change and become like little children,
you will never enter the kingdom of heaven.
~Matthew 18:3

The start of a new school year always brings a return to routine at my house. It's the same routine practiced all across the country: roust the children out of bed, make sure everyone has eaten, check to see that the five-year-old has her shoes on, see that hair and teeth are brushed, distribute lunches or lunch money, grab the book bags, and race for the door. Little thought is required for routine. As a mom, I just get in the zone and get it all done. The mental clock is usually ticking the whole time.

One recent morning proved an exception. "The trees are dancing!" exclaimed the five-year-old as we pulled out of the driveway. Her conversation about dancing trees and their choreography went on for about two minutes before I finally came out of my "accomplish the routine" mindset and noticed the amount of wind that day.

Oh! The trees were dancing! I was so busy with my routine that I failed to notice the world around me. Once I started paying attention to the movement of the leaves and the beauty of the trees "dancing," it changed my whole mindset.

Experiencing life through the eyes of a five-year-old brought beauty and appreciation back to my morning. I often find it easy to lose the sense of wonder for God's creation that I had as a child. The same is true of my relationship with God. The longer I've been in "the routine," the more likely I am to lose some of the wonder, the awe, and the freshness. It took a young child to remind me that I need to stop and enjoy the wonder of my relationship with God and His creation.

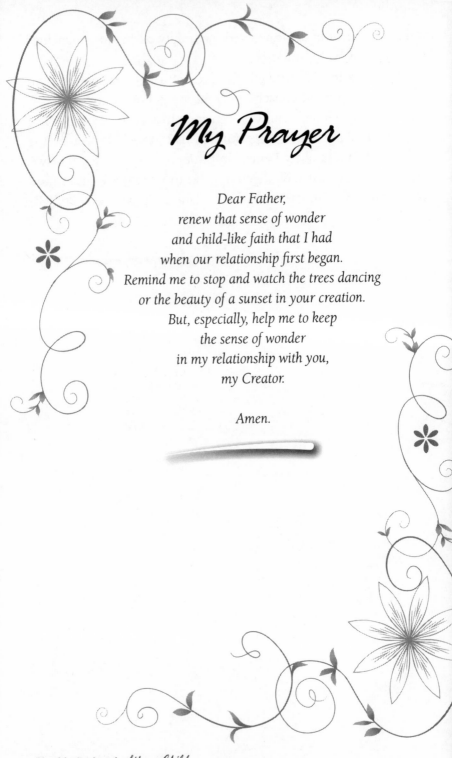

My Prayer

Dear Father,
renew that sense of wonder
and child-like faith that I had
when our relationship first began.
Remind me to stop and watch the trees dancing
or the beauty of a sunset in your creation.
But, especially, help me to keep
the sense of wonder
in my relationship with you,
my Creator.

Amen.

"Mommy, I think dancing with the trees is Nature's version of Dancing with the Stars, and we're the winners!"

17

Jesus Loves the Little Children

By Karen Talcott

For I was hungry and you gave me something to eat...
I was sick and you looked after me.
~Matthew 25:35-36

They started at 3:00 A.M.—those noises that can wake you up from the soundest of sleep. One of my children was throwing up in bed. I rushed out of my bed and across the house in seconds flat. My poor daughter was sitting up in her bed, wailing, with evidence of last night's dinner all around her. I immediately began to comfort her, clean up the mess, and try to control the situation.

When a simple virus hits my house, I often lose all perspective. I go on about all the awful symptoms and how it is so rough on our family. But the truth of the matter is that my child will get better. Yet, there are so many children in the world who have no medical care. They live in extreme poverty where medical services are not even heard of. Their mothers sit over their beds praying that they won't die from malaria, cholera, or any other curable disease in the United States.

It is during these times that I wish God would shake my shoulders a bit and lecture me about how shallow I am when there are so many other children in worse conditions. We are blessed with such a loving God, but how He must be disappointed in me some days.

When I pray for my children, I realize I need to make it a habit to also send prayers to other children in the world. As I pray that my children will grow and find their place in this world, I must also send prayers for the well-being of the billions of faceless children worldwide.

The familiar Sunday school song comes to mind, "Red or yellow, black or white, they are precious in His sight. Jesus loves the little children of the world." Let me do my part to also love these beloved children of the world.

My Prayer

God,
help me to remember
that I am a mother
to all of your beloved children.
Help me to follow the ways of Jesus
and remember that the children come to you first.
Call me to action where it is needed
to care for those who can use my help.

Amen.

18

Destiny

By Janis Bonnie

*Sons are a heritage from the Lord,
children a reward from Him.*
~Psalm 127:3

My husband and I tried for about a year and a half to get pregnant. We went through one round of in vitro fertilization and got pregnant, but lost it at about three weeks. We talked about domestic adoption, but feared falling in love with a child and then having the birth parents change their minds.

One day, my father-in-law took me to an agency that specializes in international adoption, and we were shown videos of some children who were up for adoption. The first video I saw was of a little boy from Russia who was 8-10 months old. I fell in love with him!

I took the video, two pictures, and an application home and showed them to my husband. Looking at the little boy in the picture, my husband said, "He's got Grandpa's ears!" He was referring to my grandfather, who had recently passed away. Needless to say, we filled out the application and started our journey toward adopting our son.

As the process went along, there seemed to be so many coincidences, or signs of destiny, as I called them. My son's birth mother's birthday was the same day as my mother's. The information provided about the child was done on my birthday. We kept asking for an update on his weight and height, etc., and finally received it on my mother-in-law's birthday. We went to court in Russia on my husband's birthday. But to me, the biggest confirmation of all occurred on the day before we left for Russia. We finally received the rocking chair we had been waiting for from my grandfather (the one who recently passed away).

I always tell my son he was my destiny. I found a photo album that I use as his scrapbook, and the word DESTINY is written on it, along with the saying, "If I could sit across the porch from God, I'd thank Him for lending me you."

All children are God's gift to us, no matter how they become part of our lives. Three short years later, God blessed us with another gift—our daughter, also from Russia. Although there weren't as many signs of destiny there, I truly believe she was meant to be our daughter, too.

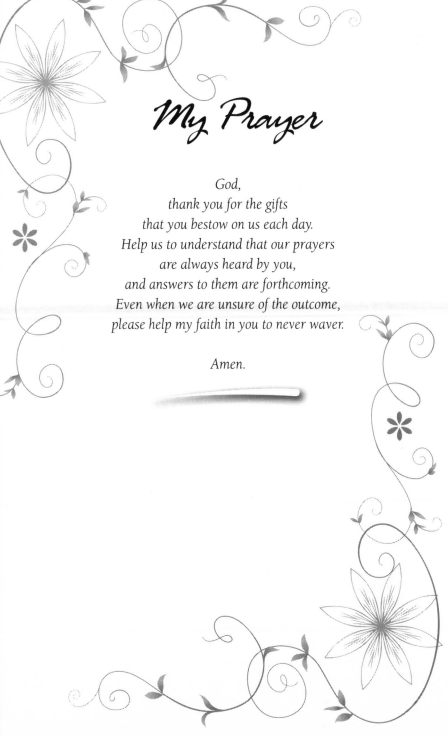

My Prayer

God,
thank you for the gifts
that you bestow on us each day.
Help us to understand that our prayers
are always heard by you,
and answers to them are forthcoming.
Even when we are unsure of the outcome,
please help my faith in you to never waver.

Amen.

In God's Hands

By Loretta D. Schoen

We went through fire and water, but you brought us to a place of abundance.
~Psalm 66:12

My daughter, Francesca, developed an eating disorder. The need to control coupled with her need to be "perfect" eventually threatened to destroy her life. I did what any caring mother would do—I yelled, cried, pleaded, reasoned, threatened, negotiated, bribed, and generally created what my daughter called "The Food Wars"! Nothing worked, not even eight weeks at a rehabilitation center.

One day, Francesca came into my office, smiling and joyful, full of life. The dichotomy of her spirit with her appearance was so apparent that I began to cry. She was so incredibly thin; she looked old and sickly.

"Francesca," I told her, "you are killing yourself, and I can do nothing to stop it. If you continue this way, you will die."

She replied, "I don't want to die, Mom."

I told her, "I believe you, honey, but that is what is going to happen. But after five years, I've realized that I can't stop you. No more fighting, and no more nagging. I will just love you and pray for you.

I cannot control this. I never could, and I know this now. The only one who can make the change is you with God's help."

Francesca began to cry, and we held each other in love and surrender.

My daughter's eating disorder wasn't instantly eliminated in that moment of surrender, but it was a catalyst for change. Our relinquishing control and accepting God as the ultimate healer allowed her to change her behavior and seek medical attention. And it allowed me to accept and have faith in God the Father.

Today, Francesca is healthy and has a beautiful baby boy. In giving control to God, she regained a healthy life and has given life! She is full of grace and thanksgiving, and cannot wait to teach her son about God, the great healer!

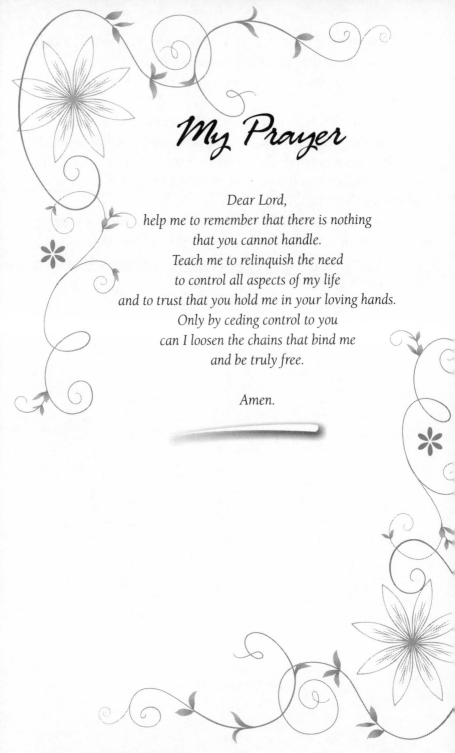

My Prayer

Dear Lord,
help me to remember that there is nothing
that you cannot handle.
Teach me to relinquish the need
to control all aspects of my life
and to trust that you hold me in your loving hands.
Only by ceding control to you
can I loosen the chains that bind me
and be truly free.

Amen.

The Best Christmas Gift

By Susan M. Heim

... and she gave birth to her firstborn, a son.
~Luke 2:7

My oldest "baby" is nineteen now, but for all his wisdom he doesn't believe he was the best Christmas present I ever received—even though I've told him numerous times. The eighties were drawing to a close, and I was expecting my baby around November 30, 1989. This would be a very special Thanksgiving for our family. We planned to have the turkey dinner at my house so I could be close to the hospital, and everyone helped out with the cooking so I didn't have to do too much.

But Thanksgiving came and went, November passed into December, and still there was no baby. My belly grew rounder and rounder, but my little firstborn seemed content to stay huddled inside. After all, it was unusually cold that year for a Florida winter!

Eleven days into December, I received a call from my doctor. "This baby may be trying to greet Jesus on his birthday," he said, "but I think we'd better give him a little nudge." So, the next morning, I waddled into the hospital and delivered my beautiful almost-Christmas baby. An enormous 9 pounds, 13-1/2 ounces, he was perfect in every way... just as I always imagined the little baby Jesus had been.

Dylan's arrival just two weeks before Christmas put a little kink in my preparations for that year, but nobody seemed to mind. He was my parents' very first grandchild, so he was their best Christmas present, too! I have no idea what presents were beneath the tree that year, but every December our family celebrates the best gift that God ever gave our family at Christmastime—our very own Christmas baby to love.

My Prayer

Dear God,
may we always remember
the true gifts of Christmas—
your Son, Jesus,
and the gathering of family and friends
to celebrate this miraculous birth.
Thank you for this tremendous gift,
born out of your great love for us.

Amen.

Chicken Soup for the Soul

Everyday Mundane Things

By Elizabeth Fenn

Whatever things you ask in prayer, believing, you will receive.
~Matthew 21:22

It was a typical Bible study evening when we would all gather together to learn more about God and how He loves us. Before the guests arrived at our house, I was trying hard to get into the right frame of mind to worship Him, but my heart was beating fast, spit-up was on my shirt, and I was in a light sweat from preparing to host our small group. My husband and I had just accomplished preparing and eating dinner, picking up toys, doing dishes, bathing our three kids, and getting them all to bed before our first guest arrived at 7:30 P.M.... and, I might add, in twenty minutes flat!

During our prayer time in the living room, I listened to the other women share with us about their struggles, hurts, and convictions. One woman was afflicted with a serious illness. Another was going through a divorce. A few had relationship woes. And a young woman was dealing with fertility issues. Again, my heart raced, but this time it was because I felt like I had nothing to share.

What was on *my* mind? Well, my two-year-old son cried off and on all day, and had a tantrum in the middle of a busy street as we were walking my daughter to preschool. My four-year-old daughter continually tested her limits in her obedience to me as a parent, in play with her brother, and in her speech. My ten-month-old had his fourth ear infection and had thrown up all over me several times that day. Who wanted to hear about my day?

I began to cry when my time came to share because my woes seemed so insignificant compared to the other women in my group. Honestly, I was struggling physically and emotionally as a parent and needed encouragement and prayer from my group. I was exhausted and needed the help of my Savior to get me through. I was quickly reminded by these dear women that the "mountain" I was climbing was just as important as what they were going through.

We often forget to call upon the Lord to help us get through the day, even when it is dealing with a temper tantrum, a growing four-year-old who is testing her independence, or a sick child. It was a wake-up call for me to remember that I don't have to be going through a major life crisis to ask the Lord for strength and perseverance in the everyday mundane things. God can do all things... even stop a temper tantrum mid-throw!

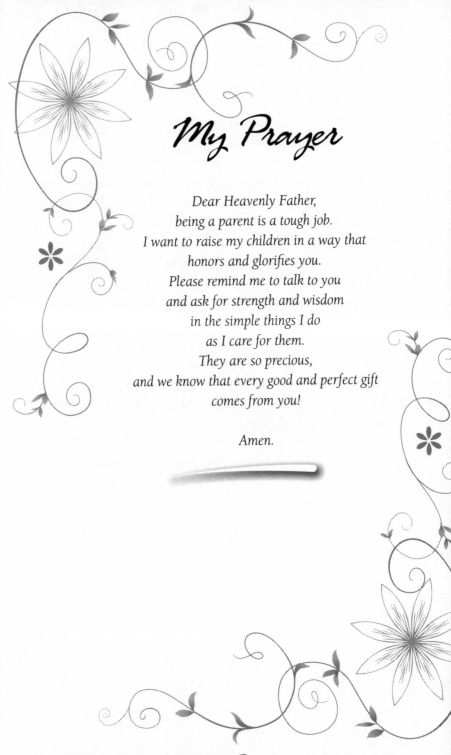

My Prayer

Dear Heavenly Father,
being a parent is a tough job.
I want to raise my children in a way that
honors and glorifies you.
Please remind me to talk to you
and ask for strength and wisdom
in the simple things I do
as I care for them.
They are so precious,
and we know that every good and perfect gift
comes from you!

Amen.

Devotional Stories for Women

Life Lessons

*I can do everything
through him
who gives me strength.*

~Philippians 4:13

Only Five Dollars

By Kimberly Kenney

The Lord does not look at things man looks at.
Man looks at the outward appearances,
but the Lord looks at the heart.
~1 Samuel 16:7

It was a busy day, and I was just trying to get my shopping done quickly. I meant to get in and out of the store with few distractions. As I approached my car, I was caught totally off-guard when a woman in her sixties came out between two cars and asked for money. She was in bad shape.

My immediate reaction was fear because she startled me. You never know what people's intentions are, so I held up my hand and said, "Sorry." She smiled and walked away.

Once I got to my car, I decided I really wanted to help this woman. I got out my wallet, called her over and handed her a $5 bill. I told her to please take care of herself, and she thanked me and started to walk away. But as I was putting the rest of my packages in my trunk, she called out to me again.

She held out her hand with the money in it and said, "Ma'am, do you realize you just gave me a $5 bill? I don't think you meant to do that."

She was planning to give it back to me because she couldn't imagine that I would have wanted to help her in that way. I told her that I absolutely meant to give it to her and that I wanted her to take care of herself by getting some food and rest. With a shocked look on her face, she smiled again and walked away. By the time I got into my car and looked for her, she was gone.

I wanted to cry. I couldn't believe that a woman so desperate was willing to give up the $5 because she thought I wouldn't want to help her. It really hit me, and I felt God speaking into my heart. Every single person deserves a chance. I was amazed at how such a small act on my part could have such a huge effect on me!

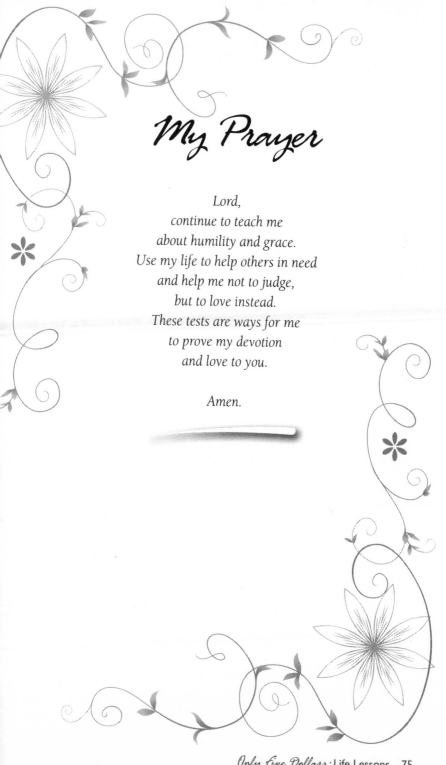

My Prayer

Lord,
continue to teach me
about humility and grace.
Use my life to help others in need
and help me not to judge,
but to love instead.
These tests are ways for me
to prove my devotion
and love to you.

Amen.

Weeding in God's Garden

By Karen Talcott

The land produced vegetation:
plants bearing seed according to their kinds
and trees bearing fruit with seed in it
according to their kinds.
And God saw that it was good.
~Genesis 1:12

I planted Ruella, a purple flowering plant, in my front flowerbed about three years ago. It looked wonderful in the store, and one of the workers told me that the maintenance on it would be minimal. So, with gusto, I planted it all over my front flowerbed. It looked great for the first year or so, and I liked how it was filling in all the empty gaps between the other plants.

Fast forward a couple of years, and I now detest this intrusive flowering plant with a passion only true gardeners know! It spread and it spread, popping up in my grass, in the sidewalk, and all over the flowerbed. It was a pretty purple *weed*! A gardener's nightmare, and now, especially, mine.

After talking to a landscape expert, I found out that the only way to remove this plant was to dig it out with a shovel. So my husband, the kids, and I set out digging. We worked one Saturday afternoon for hours. Finally, we called it a day. We pulled out huge mounds of it and felt like we had accomplished something.

Yet, this was only the beginning. The bigger problem was that every stick, twig, and root that was left in the soil could regenerate and begin to grow again. And it did!

So it came to be that I had a conversation with God as I sat there sifting through mountains of dirt looking for small pieces of the Ruella.

"God, why am I out here? My back aches, and I am so hot and tired. Can't you help me out in some way?"

There was no answer from God, so I began to mutter under my breath, "I hate you, plant. I hate you and all your roots!"

Taking a moment to wipe away my sweat, I sat back in the dirt. At that moment, the light bulb turned on. I saw God's wonderful creation—planet Earth—and it, too, was filled with weeds. But the weeds were not of the plant variety. We humans were the weeds in God's garden.

Many of us have taken for granted the beautiful world that He created in seven glorious days. Our violence, anger, and environmental destruction have taken a toll on His beloved creation. I paused to think, "Does God mutter under His breath as He tries to clean up His garden?" Knowing the answer, I thanked God for this beautiful day and the magnificent world that He so lovingly created.

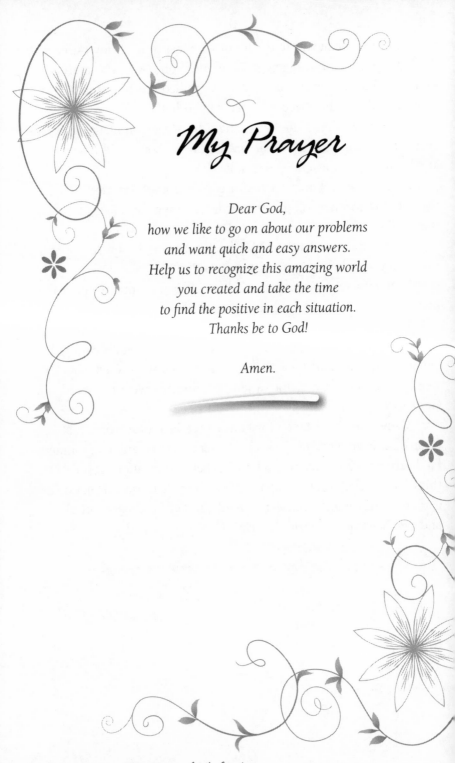

My Prayer

Dear God,
how we like to go on about our problems
and want quick and easy answers.
Help us to recognize this amazing world
you created and take the time
to find the positive in each situation.
Thanks be to God!

Amen.

" As long as you recognize that I'm the alpha weed in this garden... I think we can find a way to live together!"

Outside Our Comfort Zone

By Julie Cruz

I can do everything through him who gives me strength.
~Philippians 4:13

I stepped out of my comfort zone to lead a small group in my home. I realized I might have to start our group with prayer, and I was a little anxious. I have always prayed in my heart, but I have been shy about praying out loud. I knew this was something that God wanted me to work on, but I resisted. Of course, He insisted, as He does when He wants us to learn and grow!

The people who signed up for my small group just happened to be strong prayer leaders, so I thought, "Great, I'm off the hook!"

However, God informed me, "No, Julie, you are going to lead them in prayer."

So I called on Him for words and guidance, and I was able to pray out loud with encouragement from these amazing women.

The next day, I was with my son at a restaurant. He always prays for us before we eat, but this time, out of the blue, he said, "Mom, will you pray?"

I bowed my head and prayed, knowing with amazement that God was nudging me again (in a safe place) to pray out loud.

Then, to my complete amazement, my friend asked me to fill in for her at Parents in Prayer at our school. I wanted to say, "No, I'm not good at praying out loud," but I said, "Okay, I'll do it."

The women at Parents in Prayer encouraged and supported me through it. And God was right there with His hands on me. I realized how loving He was to place me right where I needed to be. This made me remember something a friend once told me: "The will of God will never take you to where the grace of God will not protect you."

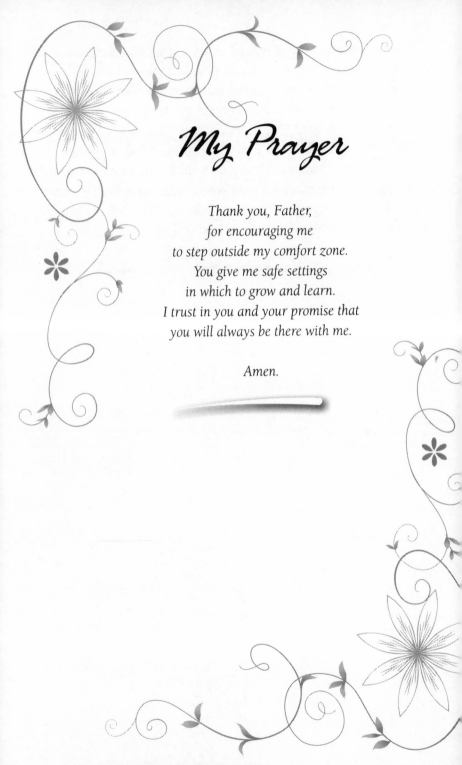

My Prayer

Thank you, Father,
for encouraging me
to step outside my comfort zone.
You give me safe settings
in which to grow and learn.
I trust in you and your promise that
you will always be there with me.

Amen.

25

The Turquoise Shoes

By Susan M. Heim

If any of you lacks wisdom,
he should ask God,
who gives generously to all without finding fault,
and it will be given to him.
~James 1:5

When I saw the turquoise shoes in the newspaper ad, I just had to have them. I had several outfits with turquoise in them, and those shoes would be the perfect accompaniment. Even better, they were marked down to $14.99, a significant reduction from their original $35 price tag. However, the store was quite a distance from my house, so I checked their website for the shoes. To my dismay, the deal was only for in-store shoppers. All that week, I checked the website to see if they'd be marked down, but they never were.

A few weeks later, I noticed that the shoes had gone on sale again! This time, I was going to be near the store on another errand, so I popped in to get them. Can you believe they were out of the turquoise shoes? They had the same shoe in black, red and white, but I had my heart set on turquoise.

When I got home, I checked the website again. This time, they were on sale! I cheerfully selected the shoes, plugged in my credit card information and got to the "checkout." I couldn't believe my eyes: "These shoes are out of stock," it said. I was so obsessed with those shoes that I checked the website again and again over the next few weeks.

Finally, they were in stock, and I was able to order them at the sale price. Unfortunately, those "perfect" shoes turned out to be the most uncomfortable pair in my closet! All that effort to get them, and I had blisters after wearing them for just a half-hour.

Have you ever set your mind on having something, certain that it was meant for you, even though all the signs were telling you it wasn't? Perhaps you stayed in a relationship with someone despite the red flags that kept popping up in warning against it. Or maybe you bought an expensive car despite the little voice in your head telling you it would put a serious dent in your budget. Consider the possibility that these signs (or red flags or internal voices) may be divine nudges about the path you should take. The next time you have a decision to make, whether it's as simple as buying shoes or as serious as purchasing a house, be still and listen to the guidance you receive from God.

My Prayer

Dear Lord,
help me to recognize your voice.
When I have a decision to make,
please remind me to ask for your guidance first,
as you always have my welfare in mind.
Thank you for taking an interest
in every choice I make,
big or small.

Amen.

" These are the worst shoes
ever. Funny how I didn't
notice the red flags in
the shoe store!"

26

Chicken Soup
for the Soul

The Parking Lot Mishap

By Andrea Federman

And the word of the LORD came again to Zechariah:
"This is what the LORD Almighty says:
'Administer true justice;
show mercy and compassion to one another.
Do not oppress the widow or the fatherless,
the alien or the poor.
In your hearts do not think evil of each other.'"
~Zechariah 7:8-10

I was late, as usual. A friend of mine had invited me to a spiritual conference, and I had been circling the parking lot for a good fifteen minutes. My mind was racing. Did the kids eat breakfast? Was my husband able to find the clothes I laid out for them? And, more importantly, would he have enough patience to look for a parking spot in this jungle of cars in order to meet me here with the kids later on?

Trying to go through the possible scenarios in my mind, I suddenly spotted a parking space. Since there was not much room, I decided to back up my giant minivan between the two white lines so the getaway would be easier after the conference had ended.

As I put my car into reverse and started driving backward, another car came out of nowhere and attempted to take my parking spot. I signaled to the driver that I was about to back up into the space, but she squeezed by me and parked her SUV in *my spot*! I couldn't believe her audacity! It made me so upset that I got out of my car and confronted the lady. By the way she was dressed, I could tell she was on her way to the conference.

I shouted at her, "That was not very angelic behavior!"

Much to my dismay, she completely ignored me, and I stormed off.

After a few minutes, I did find another parking space... behind a smelly dumpster and about a mile away from the conference (or so it seemed). Once I calmed myself down and tried to view the incident from a different angle, the possibility entered my mind that the woman may have needed the spot more than I did.

Later, I noticed she was actually one of the vendors at the conference. She must have been desperate to get there quickly in order to set up her booth and display her merchandise.

My Prayer

Dear Lord,
we are sometimes quick to judge people
or jump to conclusions
without being aware of the bigger picture.
When things seem frustrating
or stressful to us, please help us to
shine a positive light on a person or situation
and cast it in such a way
that it reflects an image
of better understanding.

Amen.

Trust in the Lord...
No Matter What

By Charlene F. Gossett

Trust in the Lord with all your heart
and lean not on your own understanding;
in all your ways acknowledge Him
and He will make your path strong.
~Proverbs 3:5-6

was working for a bank when it was announced that they would be merging with a competing bank. I had spent eight years as a faithful employee, and at first I was upset about the possibility of losing my job. I had recently purchased a new vehicle and begun making payments on the loan. I found myself allowing my mind to take flight with worry and panic, sending me on an emotional roller-coaster ride. As a Christian, I knew that God was on my side, but I wasn't trusting Him like I knew I should. I had to find a way to settle my mind and find peace about my situation.

One Sunday at church as I listened to my pastor preach a sermon, I realized that my focus had become misplaced. What I was going through wasn't about me; it was all about God. I was trying to do things my way instead of keeping my eyes on God.

I knew I had to surrender my situation to Him, giving Him total control, and let Him do His good work. I couldn't do it on my own. I needed to trust God with all of my heart, not just a little bit here or there. It's not easy to take our eyes off a difficult situation and look to God, but once we give up control to Him, we can expect to see change.

My work in the corporate world has ended, but my work for the kingdom of God will never end. I continue to be a work in progress, learning every day to trust in the Lord with all my heart. God has opened doors of opportunity to allow new and wonderful experiences into my life. Taking that step of faith wasn't easy, but the blessings made it worth the effort.

My Prayer

Dear Lord,
I trust you with all my heart.
When it seems that a door is closing in my life,
help me to see that you always
have another door open.
Guide me to keep my focus on you
and to know that you
are always looking out for me.

Amen.

28

Learning to Relinquish Control

By Jacqueline M. Gaston

God opposes the proud, but gives grace to the humble.
~James 4:6

When I learned I was expecting twins, I was bound and determined to have everything under control. I had the schedules; I had the color-coded clipboards to implement those schedules; I had all the parenting books to refer to; and, I had the baby gear. I was going to be one of those mothers who did it all.

I would work fulltime as well as be a fulltime mother and manager of the household. I was going to maintain my friendships, keep a clean house, cook nutritious meals that everyone would eat without fuss, organize play dates, and take the kids on community outings. Through all of this, I would keep my sanity and look fantastic!

Truthfully, I had a meltdown on the second day back to work. I was balancing the aspects over which I had perceived control in the safe environment of my home, but I did not have that luxury at work.

It became apparent rather quickly that maintaining the household and my career were impossible at the level that I had set for myself. I could not be the teacher and employee that I was before my twins arrived while continuing to be the mother that I had become. Since staying at home was not a financial option for our family, I had to succumb to letting go of my professional aspirations for my familial responsibilities. Initially, I perceived this as failure, but I later learned it was a lesson in humility.

Doing it all perfectly is no longer my priority; just doing what is right for my family is. Now that the twins are exploring the preschool years, I am reminded daily that control is an illusion. The house is never as clean as I had imagined, and meals are chaotic at best. Temper tantrums, public outings, and illnesses remind me that I could not possibly be as clairvoyant as I had planned. But now I'm okay with not having total control. As we get through each day, I realize who *really* has control over everything.

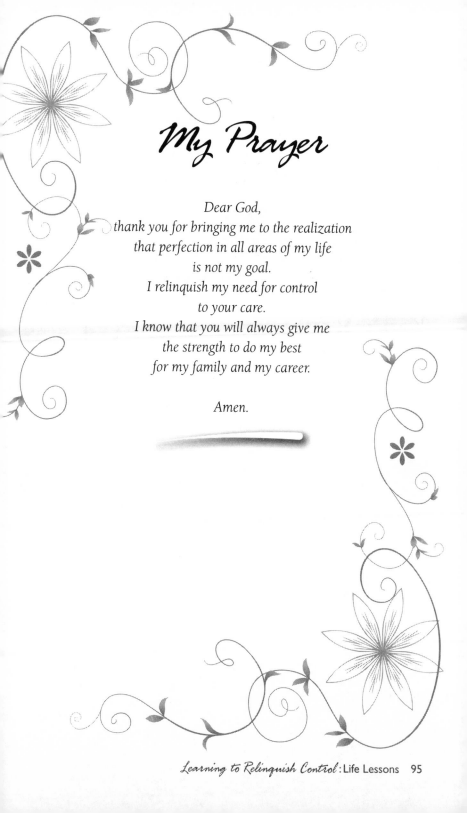

My Prayer

Dear God,
thank you for bringing me to the realization
that perfection in all areas of my life
is not my goal.
I relinquish my need for control
to your care.
I know that you will always give me
the strength to do my best
for my family and my career.

Amen.

" Compared to a happy family...
perfection can be overrated!"

29

The Rhythm of Summer

By Karen Talcott

This is the day the Lord has made;
let us rejoice and be glad in it.
~Psalm 118:24

We had been counting down the days to summer vacation, and it had finally arrived. No more cold lunches to pack, no more nights spent checking homework, and no more early morning alarms. Life was about to get a whole lot sweeter.

But, of course, if I have one plan in mind, the opposite is almost always certain to occur. The kids all roused from their beds at 7:00 A.M., hungry and wanting breakfast. By 9:00, they were already bored and looking for me to start "Mommy Camp." Wasn't summer about sipping ice-cold lemonade in a hammock under the shade of a lovely oak tree? I guess not when you are the mother of three.

But after a few days, we began to discover our summer vacation rhythm. The kids started to find things to amuse themselves. Climbing a tree and swinging down from a rope was absolutely thrilling for my five-year-old son. My daughter loved having a pretend tea party for her stuffed animals, serving them soggy crackers and water from her tea set. We didn't need to fill our time with busy theme parks and expensive attractions. Fun could be found in our own backyard or nearby park.

In my life as a mother, wife, and woman, it is so easy to get caught up in the drama of life. I micro-manage my life and fill every waking hour with things to do. What if I spent a day or two and started to notice the little things going on around me that could bring me joy?

Challenge yourself today to become more childlike. Look at this magnificent world that God created and find the wonderment in it. Laugh often, smile more, and appreciate all the beauty that exists around you. This is the day the Lord has made. Let us rejoice and be glad in it!

My Prayer

Dear God,
what a rich and wonderful world
we are blessed to live in!
You give me the amazing ability
to recognize and feel joy.
Fill my vision today
so that I may notice all the beauty
that lurks in every corner.

Amen.

Devotional Stories for Women

Illness

*But I will sing of your strength,
in the morning I will sing of your love;
for you are my fortress,
my refuge in times of trouble.*

~Psalm 59:16

The Rainbow's Promise

By Lisa Murphy

Let us hold unswervingly to the hope we profess,
for He who promised is faithful.
~Hebrews 10:23

As a healthy, active wife and mother of two young children, we were shocked to discover after a fainting spell that I had a tumor in my gastrointestinal tract. All of the tests indicated that the tumor was adhered to the lining of my small intestines. A major surgery that would entail disassembling the entire area and dissecting my pancreas was needed. The doctors could not say if it was malignant or not. Either way, chances were high I would end up diabetic after the surgery.

I prayed to God, "I will love you no matter what. I will praise you no matter what. And, if this has to happen for your glory, I am so honored you chose me."

Friends, family and our church put me on prayer lists. The church held a prayer service for me two days before the surgery. I remember the pastor saying, "Father, please leave the surgeons scratching their heads." As we all left the church, a giant rainbow was painted across the sky—a promise.

On the morning of the surgery, I was given a card with a rainbow.

As we drove to the hospital, a full rainbow was over the city. I awoke from the surgery to find the doctor smiling with two thumbs up.

He said the tumor was nothing like they had anticipated. The surgery was a simple two-and-a-half-hour procedure instead of a complicated five-to-eight-hour procedure. Best of all, because the tumor was on a stem and not adhered to the lining, my pancreas was unaffected, and it didn't matter if it was cancer. I could expect a full recovery.

"By the way," the doctor said, "you have the best room in the house."

God had provided a huge room with a kitchenette, desk, and sofa. My husband stayed many nights, and my girlfriends took turns staying with me often. It was amazing to watch God's work from my hospital bed. He used other people's previous struggles to help me, and He used my past and present to help them. One woman had been thinking of suicide, but something happened in that room to change that. Although it was an uncomfortable time, the whole experience was beautiful, and I thank God for allowing me to have it.

My Prayer

Father,
you use all things for good
for those who love you.
Thank you for all of my experiences,
the joyful and the difficult.
Thank you for loving me.
Help me to always see your hand at work
and to trust in you always.

Amen.

God Was at the Wheel

By Nancy Kershaw

Praise be to the God...
the Father of compassion and the God of all comfort,
who comforts us in all our troubles,
so that we can comfort those in any trouble
with the comfort we ourselves have
received from God.
~2 Corinthians 1:3-4

As my husband and I sat in church on the Sunday before Thanksgiving, we listened to the traditional message about giving thanks to God for our many blessings. This sermon was especially meaningful as I thought back over the past year.

In late March, my husband, daughter and I were driving home from a wedding through the mountains to our rural hometown. I fell asleep in the passenger seat, and my next memory was being in a rehabilitation center ten days later with a broken pelvis and ribs, collapsed lung and traumatic brain injury. My husband and daughter were treated and released for minor injuries.

I was confined to home and a wheelchair for two months. Without the support of our church family and community, I would have spent much longer in the rehabilitation center, but they took over sitting with me during the day while my husband was at work, providing meals and praying for our recovery.

Through the prayers and support of our family, friends and community, I am back at work part-time (much earlier than the doctors predicted). For me, the biggest challenge was having to rely on others to take care of daily tasks, such as grocery shopping and meal preparation.

This unexpected accident changed our lives, yet we all emerged stronger. My son learned to be responsible for getting his schoolwork done by himself. My daughter learned the value of a church family, and that she could keep going and finish her college semester far away from home. My husband and I remembered the value of family and friends during tough times. Through this experience, I've learned the power of prayer, and that even though God provides challenges, we become stronger in meeting them.

My Prayer

Father,
thank you for my life
and all the blessings you have given me.
Even in times of crisis,
you are there to help heal the situation.
When our bodies are weak,
you find miraculous ways to comfort us
and give us the strength to go on.

Amen.

32

A Cart full of Costco Products

By Loretta D. Schoen

Man does not comprehend its worth;
it cannot be found in the land of the living.
~Job 28:13

My mother loved going to Costco, but cancer was slowly destroying her body, and she became dependent on a wheelchair for mobility. Regardless, she was determined to stay active for as long as she could.

So, Mom and I devised a way for her to go to Costco. I would put her in her wheelchair and find a flatbed cart. She would push the flatbed cart, and I would push her. It took a little practice, but before long we were like a well-oiled machine! I pushed her, she pushed the cart; I stopped, she stopped! We even got the turns down smoothly.

One day, I parked the van on the side of the Costco building rather than in front as I usually did. After our shopping was done, we started to leave the building. In order to return to where the car was parked, we had to make a sharp left turn, avoiding the large columns in front of the building. However, the sidewalk in front of the building and around the side was on a slant. (Funny, I had never noticed that before!)

As I attempted to turn her wheelchair, Mom tried to turn the flatbed cart. However, because of the incline and the weight of the cart, she was unable to hold onto the cart, which began to roll forward and into the parking lot! As I saw this happening, I let go of Mom's wheelchair to recover the cart. Mom's wheelchair came precariously close to one of the columns and began going into the parking lot, too!

I let go of the flatbed cart and grabbed the wheelchair again. Then the cart continued to proceed into the packed parking lot once more. Unfortunately, no one except for my mother and I seemed to notice that she and my groceries were about to become chop suey!

Finally, in one last desperate act of super-heroism, my left hand grabbed my mother's wheelchair and my right hand grabbed the flatbed cart. I just hung there, torn between the two, until some nice man finally noticed our predicament and offered his help.

Once she got over the shock of the near-accident, my mother started to giggle. She said, "It's good to know how much I am worth—a flatbed cart full of Costco products!" Wheelchair: $175; flatbed cart filled with Costco products; $300; time with Mom: priceless!

My Prayer

Abba Father,
help me to enjoy all parts of my life,
even those that seem challenging!
Thank you for gifting us
with a sense of humor
so that we can laugh about those times
when things don't go quite the way we expect.
Help me to see the humorous side of life
as often as possible.

Amen.

No matter how crazy life gets... a sense of humor is the best defense!

finding Peace in the Midst of Pain

By Jennifer Stango

No discipline seems pleasant at the time,
but painful.
Later on, however,
it produces a harvest of righteousness
and peace for those
who have been trained by it.
~Hebrews 12:11

One year ago, I was buzzing through life with much to be thankful for. I was thirty-eight years old, had three beautiful kids, a wonderful husband, great friends, great church and great health—or so I thought. Then I felt a lump in my breast and quickly found out it was breast cancer.

In the next twelve months, I went through a double mastectomy, chemotherapy and radiation, and, of course, the loss of all of my hair! I thought my faith was pretty strong, but this shook me to the core. Fear crept in and tried to take hold, but the wonderful, faithful Christians around me wouldn't allow it.

So I grabbed on to the Lord and prayed for my mustard seed

of faith to grow and for peace that surpasses all understanding. Of course, I prayed for healing, but I knew that wasn't always God's plan. Through every test result and doctor's appointment, I prayed for God to keep me sane.

I know now that the only way I got through those twelve months was with the Lord carrying me through. Whenever I walked through the doctor's door, waiting for test results, my knees would be shaking. But I would tell myself, "He will get me through," and He always did. Somehow, through all this insanity, I was able to laugh and smile and thank God for so many things.

There was the time I cried out to the Lord, "I cannot wait five days for these test results!" and they came back two days later. And the time when I wasn't sure whether to postpone one of my surgeries for another family emergency when the doctor's office called not an hour after I prayed for guidance and asked if they could reschedule. God is so amazing!

Somehow, I found peace during this difficult time. It was hard, and cancer is scary, but I faced it because I knew that God was working in my life. I'm now done with all of my treatments and surgeries, and I can look back and know that my faith—once the size of a mustard seed—has grown. I learned that God really does give you what you need. When you go through the dark times believing in this assurance, I promise you He will.

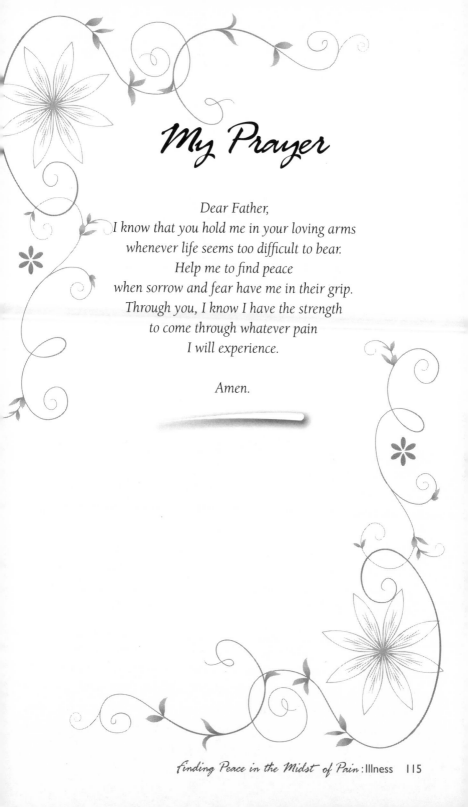

My Prayer

Dear Father,
I know that you hold me in your loving arms
whenever life seems too difficult to bear.
Help me to find peace
when sorrow and fear have me in their grip.
Through you, I know I have the strength
to come through whatever pain
I will experience.

Amen.

34

A Healing from Heaven

By Laura Bartolini Mendelsohn

Praise the LORD,
O my soul, and forget not all his benefits —
who forgives all your sins
and heals all your diseases.
~Psalm 103:2-3

As a shy seventeen-year-old, I could not wait to get home from the world-renowned Hospital for Special Surgery in New York that excruciatingly hot day in July 1970. As soon as I arrived, I leapt to my bedroom, throwing my face on my pillow, and sobbing uncontrollably. No amount of pounding fists or furious tears could change my fate. The doctors had recommended an operation that would put me in a body cast for a year and force me to learn to walk again. I was devastated.

I had been diagnosed with scoliosis (curvature of the spine) and a severe lower back injury, which could cause me to lose the ability to walk later in life. I had heard about scoliosis, but now I was the one burdened with this deformity beneath baggy clothes and a "great personality." On that hot July day, I decided there was no way I was going to have this scary operation. I would live with my twisted body and lower back pain well into young adulthood, stoically accepting my "ugly" fate.

But, since the medical establishment had no hope for me, I continued to experiment to find healing through various unorthodox treatments. For a long time, I never felt inspired to ask for help in prayer. I had pounded my fists and looked for "cures," but the pristine simplicity of prayer had evaded me. It was only when I realized that I had exhausted all of my own attempts to heal myself that I began to pray to God.

Shortly afterward, I started having dreams of being a ballerina. I quickly realized that ballerinas had magnificently straight spines, so I signed up for ballet lessons. After each lesson, I would feel and look straighter, taller and more symmetrical. My spine continued to improve.

I moved from being the quiet girl to a sought-out social butterfly. I even became an avid ballroom and Latin dancer. An entirely new social life and artistic expression blossomed around my adversity. After praying for help, I had been led by my dreams to a healing that finally worked!

My Prayer

Dear God,
you are the Great Healer,
who can mend our spiritual,
mental and physical ailments.
Please help us to remember
to include you in our treatment plans.
Only through you can we become
the full expression of ourselves that you created.

Amen.

35

Food from the Heart

By Karen Talcott

Bring the best of the first fruits of your soil
to the house of the Lord your God.
~Exodus 23:19

received a call today asking if I would be willing to bring food to a family in crisis. The mother was having major surgery and would be off her feet for several weeks. Of course, I responded with an immediate "Yes!" As I planned the meal in my head, I reflected on how many times over the years I have been asked to prepare food. I have done so countless times with such an open heart.

But the truly amazing thing is that for the number of times I have shared food, I have received double over the course of my life. When my mother passed away, our house was filled with fresh dinners for weeks. A new church member stopped by each evening with a casserole to talk and mourn with us. The gift of food was her small way of trying to ease our pain.

Later in my life, when I was on bed rest during my pregnancy with twins, women of the church again stepped in to help. They arranged babysitting for my two-year-old daughter, and brought me books to read and lovely dinners to our house. Even when I was put in the hospital, my husband would bring the home-cooked meals to my hospital room. How we relied on these dinners to feed my stressed-out husband and young daughter!

Food is all about comfort. It feeds our bodies, but it can also feed our souls. When you hear people talking about their favorite holidays, it usually includes their feelings associated with sharing food. The greatest example of this is Jesus' Last Supper. Even though he knew the crisis that awaited him, he still shared a beloved meal with his closest friends.

I know that I will have many more opportunities in my lifetime to prepare food for others. It is truly a gift I look forward to preparing and delivering to someone in need.

My Prayer

God,
from the simple act of breaking bread
to preparing food,
you give us opportunities
to show our love for others.
I pray that you will continue to
use me in this way.
Thank you for allowing me
to nurture the bodies —
and the souls —
of those in my life.

Amen.

36

Caring for My Own Health

By L.P.

God is our refuge and strength,
an ever-present help in trouble.
Therefore we will not fear.
~Psalm 46:1-2

The holidays were coming up, and I was really busy—too busy to see a doctor, I reasoned, even after I found a suspicious-looking mole. The mole was in a very unusual place on my body, so for a long time I didn't know it was there. When I did find it, I put off treatment for a million reasons, mostly because I didn't know what it was.

It turned out to be malignant and was removed. A skin sample and some lymph nodes were taken to be sure the cancerous cells had not spread. It was not exactly pleasant, but it could have been worse.

I was told that it's very common to have malignant moles in weird, hard-to-see places. We're often told to check our bodies for suspicious moles, but most people don't think to check all over the bodies. As a result, cancers in these areas are often missed. Sometimes, the only way to find them is with a small mirror. I now encourage all women, regardless of how busy they are, to put their health first.

I wondered out loud how to express my gratitude to God that Christmas, and my sons overheard me. One of them said, "Mom, I think you should get Him a candy cane. Everyone needs some sweetness in their life." So there you have it... for those hard-to-shop-for people on your list, a simple candy cane should do the trick. And maybe a small mirror...

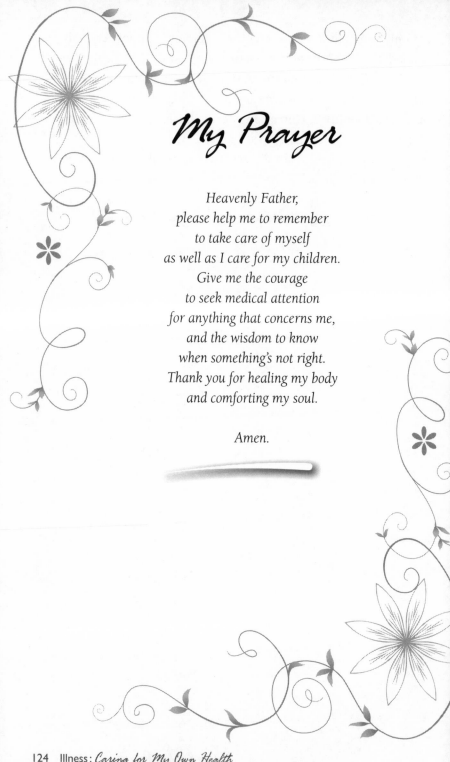

My Prayer

Heavenly Father,
please help me to remember
to take care of myself
as well as I care for my children.
Give me the courage
to seek medical attention
for anything that concerns me,
and the wisdom to know
when something's not right.
Thank you for healing my body
and comforting my soul.

Amen.

37

For Everything There Is a Season

By Sandra Diane Stout

But those who hope in the LORD
will renew their strength.
They will soar on wings like eagles;
they will run and not grow weary,
they will walk and not be faint.
~Isaiah 40:31

Our daughter was diagnosed with a rare tumor in her hip socket. She had two major hip surgeries and spent months in therapy and a wheelchair, followed by crutches. Six months after the second surgery, we lost our barn and dairy operation in a ferocious fire. We watched in devastation as a part of history and our lives burned to the ground.

Five months later, during the clean-up and reconstruction of the barns, my husband had his right leg amputated due to a serious farm accident. While dealing with this difficult situation, I severely burnt my right hand. I was afraid of how this would affect my ability to play the piano, my life's passion. Due to overuse of my left hand, I had carpal tunnel surgery. Things started to get back to "almost" normal when certain events and difficult situations caused our family to leave our home church.

I felt like I had lost everything. I had to hold on to God's promises. Even though I knew God was there and would not leave me—that He has a reason for everything—I still had moments when I cried out to Him, "Why?"

But by trusting in God, our family gained wisdom from the difficulties we experienced. Our barn and dairy were rebuilt with the help of friends and family. My husband continued farming and inspired other amputees by sharing his experience. We joined a larger church where I became the drama director and keyboardist in the Faith Praise Ensemble. Our daughter's experience led her to finish her master's degree as a radiologist assistant.

When our faith is tested, it teaches endurance and equips us with strength for tomorrow. God specializes in using our trials to prepare us to accomplish the awesome!

My Prayer

Heavenly Father,
you are a great God.
As I meet today's trials and frustrations,
give me renewed awareness
of your constant, loving presence.
May I not forget that
I am here to serve you.
May I use the wisdom and strength
I gain from my trials
to bring your love to those around me.

Amen.

Devotional Stories for Women

God's Helpers

*Do not forget to entertain strangers,
for by so doing some people
have entertained angels
without knowing it.*

~Hebrews 13:2

38

God's Protection

By Lorie Bibbee

If you make the Most High your dwelling—
even the Lord, who is my refuge—
then no harm will befall you, no disaster will come near your tent.
For he will command his angels concerning you
to guard you in all your ways;
they will lift you up in their hands,
so that you will not strike your foot against a stone.
~Psalm 91:9-12

hen I was twenty-something, I flew all over the country teaching small offices how to make my company's computers work for them. One night when I was traveling, it was very late by the time I got to a tiny town, and I was tired. I checked into the motel, hung up my dress, brushed my teeth and fell dead asleep in the bed.

Hours later, the phone rang. Sleepily, I listened to the man on the other end tell me that he was calling from the front desk and that I had left my credit card there. He asked me to please come and pick it up.

Without thinking, probably because I was still half-asleep, I stepped into my dress and went to unlock the door. It was dead-bolted, and when I went to close my hand over the lock, my hand couldn't touch it. I physically couldn't touch the lock! It was as though an invisible hand was covering the lock, and I could only touch the hand. I kept trying until I really woke up.

I went to my purse and found my credit card where it belonged. Then I called the front desk, and a quiet woman answered the phone. I asked if the man at the front desk had called me, and she said that the only man there was the security guard, who didn't make the call. At that point, I asked her to call the police.

I went to the door and looked out the peephole. I saw a white pickup with three men sitting in the front seat. When the police caught up with them, it was determined that they were wanted for doing some very bad things in the past.

But no evil befell me. My Lord and my God protected me. Even in my sleepy, non-thinking foolishness, He didn't allow what evil had intended. I *could not* unlock the door! I could not even touch the lock. Thankfully, being abducted by three men in a white truck was not in God's plan that night.

My Prayer

Thank you most precious and holy Lord
for being in control of our lives.
We are grateful that you never sleep
and are never taken by surprise,
for even the darkness is as light to you.
Help us to remember
that you are so much bigger
than any evil attack.

Amen.

39

Hang On and Don't Let Go

By Melody Riccardo

The Lord will protect him and preserve his life.
~Psalm 41:2

Growing up in Florida, I naturally learned to swim early. When I grew older, I became interested in surfing. I loved it right away and was determined to learn how to surf well. I did get better over time and often entered surfing contests. I managed to do well in most of them, but I soon became tired of competing. It took the fun out of it!

One day, though, I heard that a freak Arctic swell (a term for a type of wave) had arrived, and the waves were twelve to fifteen feet, clean, glassy and strong. I couldn't resist going out on those beautiful waves. I got out to where they were breaking and rode in on three separate waves. But as I paddled back out to ride more, a menacing set of waves started to roll in. I heard later that everyone watching on the beach said that it was "the set of the day."

It looked impressive from the shore, but it was downright scary in the water. The biggest wave I've ever seen approached me quickly, a mountain of water ready to crush me. I was scared and thought I was going to die. Then a deep, commanding voice inside my head or near me told me what to do to survive.

"Wrap your arms completely around the board as tight as you can. Do not let go!"

I obeyed, and the wave curled up and slammed me hard. I tumbled around and down like I was in a washing machine, but I did not let go. It felt as if the air in my lungs was about to burst. The board started to shoot up toward the surface, and I finally got some air, but I had to hold my breath again as another wave hit. Wave after wave pounded me down until they finally subsided.

After it was all over, I sat on the beach and cried. If I had done what I usually did to get past a wave, I would not be here today. The voice had saved me. Do I believe in angels? You bet! God's loving helpers protected me that day on the ocean. It is such a comfort knowing that angels are all around us and ready to help in our time of need.

My Prayer

Thank you, God,
for sending your loving helpers into our lives.
You answer all prayers, even before
we have a chance to utter them out loud.
Thank you for the heavenly protection
that you send us from above.

Amen.

" I'm never afraid to shoot the Curl of life because I know I've got Divine protection! "

40

Angels All Around

By Holly Shapiro-Robillard

For he will command his angels concerning you
to guard you in all your ways;
they will lift you up in their hands,
so that you will not strike your foot against a stone.
~Psalm 90:11-12

My son has always had a very special insight into the presence of God. *One night he witnessed my angel.* It was during an extremely difficult time in our lives. He was in kindergarten, and his father had been placed in a facility due to mental illness.

My son knew his father was ill as he had watched him progress from the dad he once knew to what seemed like a stranger among us. The doctors told me he was not responding to his medications, and I had to make some very difficult decisions concerning his care. I sought spiritual counsel and prayed for an answer. After tucking in my two small children, I would fall into bed each night, exhausted from the decisions and the despair I felt.

One evening as I was tucking in my son as usual, he said, "Mommy, last night I came into your room, and I saw your angel. He was sitting by you while you were sleeping. He wore a black shirt and had big arms. He was staring at you. I was not scared when I saw him. I just went back to sleep."

I know with all my heart that my son saw the true presence of my angel that evening. God was with us in that very moment through the faith of my young son, who was open to all God has to offer to bring peace and healing into our home.

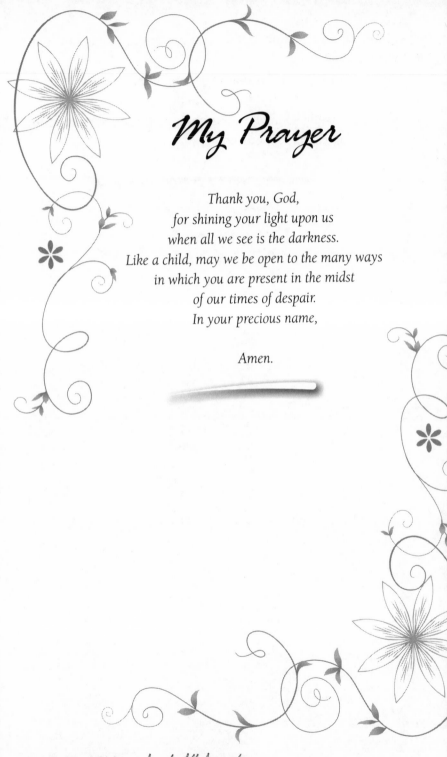

My Prayer

Thank you, God,
for shining your light upon us
when all we see is the darkness.
Like a child, may we be open to the many ways
in which you are present in the midst
of our times of despair.
In your precious name,

Amen.

God Sent Me an Angel

By Gail Frank

He protected us on our entire journey
and among all the nations through which we traveled.
~Joshua 24:17

I was raising two children by myself. My schedule was challenging as I cared for the children during the day and attended nursing school at night. On the nights I had school, I would take my children over to my mother's house. She would feed them and put them to bed. Around 11:00 P.M., I would arrive at her house and put my sleeping children in the back seat of my car. Although I was often tired and exhausted, I still had to stay awake for the thirty-minute drive back to my house.

One particular night, it was very dark, and the freeway was empty of other cars. The night seemed uneventful until, all of a sudden, I heard a pop and a thud. One of my worst fears had come true: My car tire was flat. I was alone on this stretch of the freeway, and my two sleeping children were in the back seat of the car.

Not knowing what else to do, I immediately started praying to God. "Please, God, help me now. I don't know what to do."

At that moment, a car pulled up behind mine. A young man stepped out of his car and said, "It looks like you could use a hand." Strangely, I had no fear of being in his presence.

He changed my tire rather quickly and put the old tire in my trunk. I offered to pay him, but he waved away the money. I got back into my car feeling so relieved. But when I looked up again, he was gone. There were no headlights, taillights or signs that he had been around. There weren't even any tread marks from his car on the side of the road. It was like he had vanished into thin air!

As I sat in the car saying "Thank you, God" over and over again, I realized that God had sent me an angel. This event took place more than thirty-five years ago, but it is as clear in my mind today as it was on that dark evening. My children and I were divinely protected and watched over that night.

My Prayer

God,
when times are rough,
you send us your angels
to lovingly protect us.
How great are the miracles
that you perform!
We thank you for this comfort in our lives.

Amen.

42

Comfort from the Angels

By Mary O'Reilly-Seim

My comfort in my suffering is this:
Your promise preserves my life.
~Psalm 119:50

For several years, our son has been experiencing severe and debilitating mental health issues. The previous few months had been a roller coaster nightmare for him and our entire family. I went to church for my weekly hour of prayer. As I sat alone in the church, my prayers for help, strength and guidance were offered with a waterfall of tears. Close to the end of the hour, I sat back in the pew, drained and exhausted.

Suddenly, I was surrounded with a sense of comfort that was so powerful it almost felt like a hug. At that exact moment (7:25 P.M.), the church bells in the steeple began to ring, and they rang for almost a full minute. I turned around to see who was at the bell tower control buttons. No one was there.

I knew that my angels were giving me a clear message that I

was not traveling this journey alone. In Psalm 86:17, it says, "Give me a sign of your goodness... for you, O LORD, have helped me and comforted me."

I knew in that moment that God's angels were always with me.

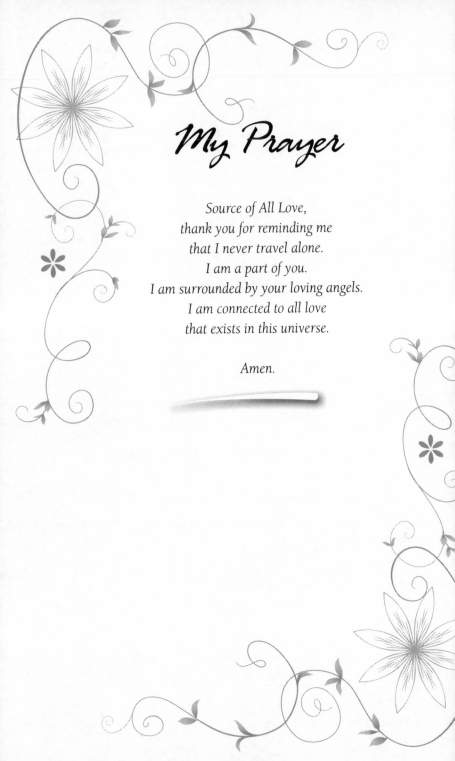

My Prayer

Source of All Love,
thank you for reminding me
that I never travel alone.
I am a part of you.
I am surrounded by your loving angels.
I am connected to all love
that exists in this universe.

Amen.

43

A Car Whizzed By

By Susan Forma

My God sent his angel,
and he shut the mouths of the lions.
~Daniel 6:22

Many years ago, I attended Drexel University in west Philadelphia. On the weekends, we'd do what most college students do — stay up late. When we would get our second wind around 11 or 12 o'clock at night, we would often drive into south Philly for a delicious Philly Cheese Steak. Most of south Philly consists of old narrow streets, some of them still cobblestone, with lots of small alleys between homes and roadways.

On one particular night, about five of us loaded into one car and went to satisfy our late-night craving. It was always busy at this steak place, and the line was quite long. Somehow, I managed to get my cheese steak before the others. Despite the many people at the window ordering sandwiches, I was alone walking back to the car. Many years ago, my cousin was hit by a truck, and it destroyed her face. Therefore, I always thought of Cousin Hannah and took extra care to look both ways time and time again before venturing off a curb.

That night, however, I thought I was just crossing an alley. I wasn't aware that it was wide enough for cars to pass through, and it certainly wasn't a usual thoroughfare for cars. Therefore, I simply stepped off the curb to cross without looking. As soon as my foot left the curb, someone grabbed me by the back of my jacket and yanked me briskly back. At that exact moment, a car full of teens went whizzing in front of me and down the alley. My heart was beating a mile a minute as I knew I had just escaped death.

I turned to see who had saved me so I could thank him, but I found myself alone. My friends were just leaving the order window with their sandwiches and were way too far away to have helped. I knew that some loving angel had just saved my life! I am so thankful that someone was watching over me.

My Prayer

Thank you, God,
for sending your angels to watch over me.
I know that you have a very important purpose
in mind for me.
Please show me what I need to do in this lifetime
so that I can fulfill all that you ask of me.

Amen.

44

Gifts from God

By Susan M. Heim

Consider how the lilies grow.
They do not labor or spin.
Yet I tell you, not even Solomon in all his splendor
was dressed like one of these.
If that is how God clothes the grass of the field,
which is here today, and tomorrow is thrown into the fire,
how much more will he clothe you,
O you of little faith!
~Luke 12:27-28

A pastor from my church was attending a conference out of town and discovered, upon arriving at his hotel, that he had forgotten his shaving materials. The hotel desk was also out of additional razors.

"Well, a day without a shave won't be too bad," the pastor told himself. "When I get a break from the meetings tomorrow, I'll dash out to the corner store and pick up some disposable razors."

Unfortunately, the next day's meetings and activities ran long, and the pastor never did get out to the store.

"Hopefully, I'll get a chance to run out the following day," he told himself.

The next day, it was the same story: no time to go out. By this point, the pastor was looking quite "scruffy" and unkempt.

On the third day of the conference, he was crossing the parking lot, when something directly in his path made him halt in his tracks. He reached down to the ground and picked up a brand-new disposable razor, still in its original packaging! Coincidence... or a gift from heaven?

How often have you run out of money, only to fish a forgotten twenty-dollar bill out of a pair of pants? Have you ever thought about a long-lost friend, when she suddenly calls you on the phone? Perhaps you've worried about how you'd be able to accomplish everything in a day, when your schedule is suddenly lightened by an unexpected appointment cancellation. Think about all the times that God or his angels have provided for you... when you didn't even realize you'd uttered a prayer!

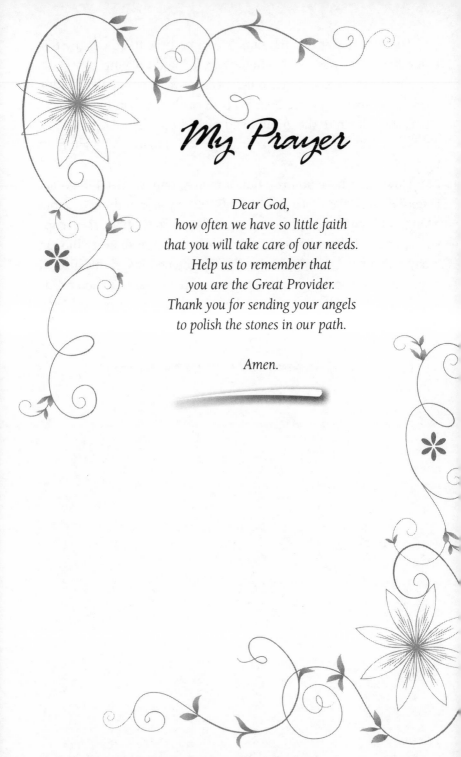

My Prayer

Dear God,
how often we have so little faith
that you will take care of our needs.
Help us to remember that
you are the Great Provider.
Thank you for sending your angels
to polish the stones in our path.

Amen.

45

You Are Never Alone

By Ingrid Michele Smith

Be merciful to me, Lord, for I am faint;
O Lord, heal me, for my bones are in agony,
My soul is in anguish,
How long, O Lord, how long?
~Psalm 6:2-3

My husband had been coming home from work every day saying that he was so stressed out and had to take a nap. This went on for a couple of months, and then he started having headaches. I was worried about him having a stroke and asked the doctor to order a CAT scan. Unfortunately, this revealed that he had a brain tumor.

The neurosurgeon told me that he would die within the year, and he had to have surgery immediately. I could not believe this was happening to us. He was fifty-seven years old, the best husband and father.

Within seven months of being diagnosed with the brain tumor, my beloved husband passed away. I was devastated, and felt so alone and sad.

One day, I was in the lunchroom at work, and one of the ladies asked me what was wrong as she could see that I was sad. The feelings were so overpowering that I just started crying and had to leave.

When I got back to my desk, I saw a beautiful white feather on my chair. I knew that it was a sign from the angels. I work in a completely enclosed building, and there is no way a feather could blow in through a window or anywhere else. I felt so much better and no longer alone in that moment.

My Prayer

Thank you, Lord,
for sending me signs that I am not alone.
Your angels are with me always,
protecting me and helping me
in my moments of loneliness.
Help me to recognize
the signs of your loving presence.

Amen.

46

His Eye Is on the Sparrow

By Carrie Ellis

Indeed, the very hairs of your head are all numbered.
Don't be afraid;
you are worth more than many sparrows.
~Luke 12:7

t was just another ordinary day, or so I thought as I drove along the interstate in the slow lane. I was on my way to my job in my usual stressed-out mode. I struggled to keep all the balls in the air while working full-time in a difficult position, being a loving wife and mother to a challenging child, and finding some time to myself. Here I was on another trip to my job, twenty-five miles from home and heading into rush-hour traffic.

"This is just what I need—a stressful ride to start my stressful job," I thought sarcastically.

I was alone in my quiet car when I felt it: a distinct smack on the back of the driver's seat. At that very moment, I was filled with heart-stopping panic and fear as the thought raced through my mind that I was not alone in the car. I picked my foot off the gas pedal in an automatic involuntary response to the fear that gripped me.

Then, as if I were in a dream, my car slowed as I watched another car from the fast lane careen across the highway just a few feet in front of me. It continued past me and off the highway, taking out a telephone pole. As I glided by, the telephone pole twirled in the air and came crashing down behind me.

Once I got past the accident, I quickly looked into my backseat. There was no one there, at least nobody that I could see.

One of my favorite Bible verses is found in Matthew 6:34: "Do not worry about tomorrow." I have read it over and over as I've struggled not to worry about things in my life. Even after the events of this day, I struggle with worry. But I have a renewed faith that I am not alone, and nothing happens without His knowing. I know that God or one of His messengers was in the car with me that day. I learned the lessons of this verse in a very personal way through His provision and came to understand that His eye is on the sparrow. I know He watches me.

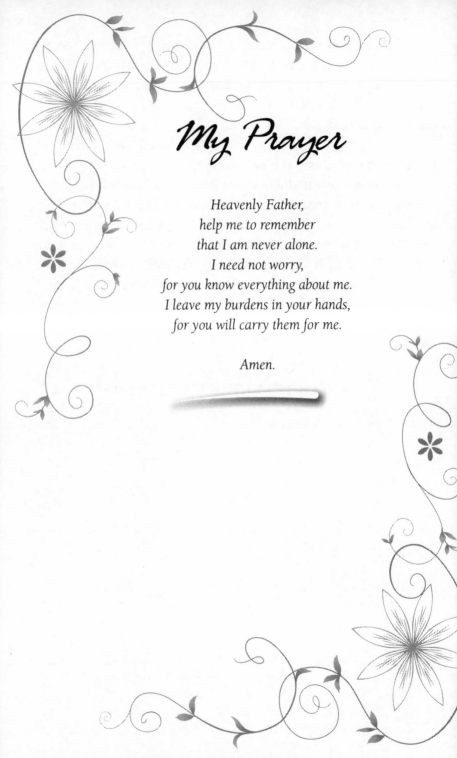

My Prayer

Heavenly Father,
help me to remember
that I am never alone.
I need not worry,
for you know everything about me.
I leave my burdens in your hands,
for you will carry them for me.

Amen.

47

A Visit from the Holy Spirit

By Jeanie McGuire Tennant

And hope does not disappoint us, because God has poured out his love into
our hearts by the Holy Spirit, whom he has given us.
~Romans 5:5

When I was a young mother, I went through a divorce. One weekend when my children were with their father, I joined a female friend at her mountain retreat. I went with a very heavy heart, confused about what was happening and where I was going. I had grown up in a Christian family, and I attended church with my children, but I was focused on me, not God.

One night as I was falling asleep in that mountain retreat, a powerful presence filled the bedroom. I was worn out and desperate.

I said aloud, "I do not know if you are good or evil, but I give up."

The next thing I remember was waking up in the sunlight of morning with a smile on my face and a sense of peace in my soul.

My life did not have a dramatic turnaround nor did things

become easier. But I knew I was not alone. My life had purpose, and there was a path to follow. All I had to do was take one step at a time and keep my feet on the path, and I would be cared for. I now know it was the Holy Spirit. I feel the joy of God's love in my heart.

My Prayer

Dear Lord,
You are more awesome than I could ever imagine.
I am blessed to know that
the Holy Spirit has been given to me
to guide me in the purpose you have for me.
I feel radiant to know that through Jesus Christ
I am forgiven and loved.

In Jesus' name, I pray.

Amen.

Devotional Stories for Women

Parenting

*He tends his flock like a shepherd:
He gathers the lambs in his arms
and carries them close to his heart;
he gently leads those that have young.*

~Isaiah 40:11

48

A Cure for the Worry Gene

By Deborah R. Albeck

I will not leave you as orphans;
I will come to you.
~John 14:18

"I found a beautiful place to sit outside and study. It's grassy, beside a small pond, and has several huge shade trees."

My daughter, Mallory, was describing to me over her cell phone a special spot she had discovered at the university she is attending. As she explained the spot in detail, I envisioned it as a lovely place.

"And, Mom, it's so quiet. Secluded behind two classroom buildings, hardly anyone comes around, and..."

What? Wait a minute! Secluded? No one around? Suddenly, I was envisioning something totally different and much more sinister. My *"what if* gene" kicked into high gear. *What if* a deranged person attacked her in this secluded place? *What if* a hungry gator was lurking in that pond? *What if* she needed help and no one was within hearing distance?

Why do I naturally "go there" with all these worries and doubts?

I must have inherited this worry gene from my father. In any stressful situation, my mother remained relatively calm while my father thought of all the horrible scenarios that might happen. And although I do believe that being cautious can prevent many ills, I also realize that long-term worrying can be as destructive as any human disease. It affects not only the worriers of the world, but all the folks who love them. Where is the dividing line between being a cautious, caring parent and teaching your kids that the world is a scary place to live?

Jesus was direct in his command for us not to worry. "Therefore do not worry about tomorrow, for tomorrow will worry about itself" (Matthew 6:34).

I am learning to use Jesus' words to fight my worry gene. Now, in any given situation, I instruct or advise my teenagers on what I feel to be the best course of action, and then I thank God for taking care of them, especially while they are living away from home. I ask God to watch over them and envision His protective arms wrapped around them. Then, and only then, can I let go. By overcoming my anxiety through prayer and faith, I spend less time fretting and more time enjoying what God has so graciously given me.

My Prayer

Dear Heavenly Father,
thank you for caring
for my children throughout the years.
Please continue to wrap your loving,
protective arms around them as they
live out their lives
more and more independently of me.

In Jesus Christ's most precious name, I pray.

Amen.

49

Feeling Like Peter

By Susan M. Heim

"I tell you the truth,"
Jesus answered,
"this very night, before the rooster crows,
you will disown me three times."
~Matthew 26:34

I felt sort of like Peter this week, and not in a good way. Remember how Peter denied his relationship with Jesus—three times in a row? Of course, afterward he felt terrible about what he'd done, but at the time, he just couldn't seem to stop himself from doing something wrong. That's how I felt. Oh, I didn't do something as bad as denying Jesus, but I failed to do the right thing when the opportunity presented itself—over and over again.

First, every day when my twins and I are driving home from preschool, Caleb asks me to take them to the park. And every day, I have a different excuse not to go. The worst one was, "Don't you want to go home and have your snack?" I was encouraging them to load up on ice cream instead of exercise!

Second, Caleb asked me to go outside and play hockey with them. "No, it's too cold," I told him. Of course, we could have just put on some jackets!

My third "sin" was almost not going to the beach today. My husband had decided to take the twins, but told me I could stay home and work if I wanted. It was a gorgeous day, but I actually debated over the decision. I thought about all the deadlines I had to meet and seriously considered sitting at the computer instead of spending a couple of hours playing with my kids at the beach. Thankfully, I came to my senses and decided to go.

If Peter can move on from his mistakes and become one of the greatest disciples of the early church, perhaps it wouldn't be so difficult for me to learn to cherish the opportunities to head to the park, take a walk, play a little hockey or go to the beach. My boys will only be four once, and we've only got one life to live in this beautiful world.

It's time to head outside and play more often. As Catherine Hickem wrote, "Embrace the journey of motherhood with the belief that you will *empower* your children to *fulfill* the purpose of their special creation."

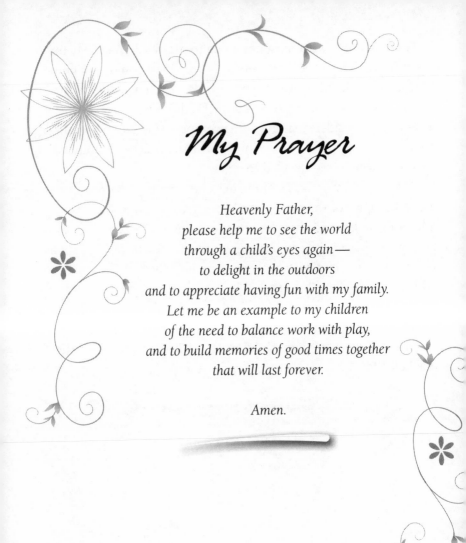

My Prayer

Heavenly Father,
please help me to see the world
through a child's eyes again—
to delight in the outdoors
and to appreciate having fun with my family.
Let me be an example to my children
of the need to balance work with play,
and to build memories of good times together
that will last forever.

Amen.

50

Training Wheels and Trust

By Karen Talcott

Therefore encourage one another and build each other up,
just as in fact you are doing.
~1 Thessalonians 5:9

The task of teaching my children to ride their bikes fell upon me. For some unspoken reason, it was easier for me than for my husband to teach the kids this important life skill. With two children down and one to go, I mentally prepared for this last battle. Announcing it was time to take off the training wheels, I watched the face of my five-year-old daughter. She wore a look of anticipation as I removed the bolts holding her extra wheels. We then wheeled the bike down the driveway for the first ride.

Checking the street for any cars, I placed her on the bike. We talked about how to control it, brake, and pedal. Then, with the first unforgettable push, I launched her down the road. She rode five feet and then crashed hard on the pavement. Gone was the look of anticipation, and in its place were tears. I rushed to comfort her and tend to her scraped knees, but I knew in my heart that they weren't going to be her only cuts that day.

We would repeat this process over and over again. Each time she made it farther down the street with me shouting words of encouragement beside her. As a parent, I had to be her cheerleader, coach, and medic. And, more importantly, I had to keep her on the bike. I knew from experience that I couldn't let her quit. She could learn to ride on her own, but it would take practice.

I have a feeling that God feels the same way about us. We live our lifetime trying new opportunities and adventures. But there are those moments when we wobble and fall down. We are hurt and scared to try again. During these times, we must put our trust in God as our heavenly parent. He cheers for our achievements, provides insight and instruction, and gently loves us through the pain.

My Prayer

God,
there are so many
new skills to learn in this world.
Please be with us when
we attempt something new
and give us the courage
to see it through to completion.

Amen.

51

Stumbling on the Path

By Gerri Kinley

He will not let your foot slip—
he who watches over you will not slumber;
indeed, he who watches over Israel
will neither slumber nor sleep.
~Psalm 121:3-4

*E*arly one morning, I was driving my daughter, Abigail, to ballet class. As usual, her younger siblings had come along. During the entire drive, the back seat of my minivan became a literal war zone. My three "angels" screamed and bickered as if their lives depended upon how high the volume could get! To make matters worse, my yelling from the driver's seat to make them stop only added to the pandemonium. My mind began to slowly drift off into a dark cloud of misery and guilt.

"I'm such a failure," I thought. "What kind of mother am I? What did I do wrong to produce this atmosphere with my children?"

In my mind, I wanted to be someplace far away. Turning on the radio was the quickest means of escape.

"Are you a mother of three, ages six and under?" said a voice from the radio. I perked up! "Do you feel angry and frustrated trying to deal with the incessant whining and fighting of toddlers? Well, you're not alone, and my guest today has something to say to you."

The guest happened to be a Christian psychiatrist eager to relate his experiences as a father.

"Every Saturday morning," the doctor began, "I give my wife a break from our kids. She leaves early in the morning and returns about midday. During this time, I feed and play with my children and attempt to get them to do their chores. My whole morning is so saturated with sibling rivalry that I find myself yearning for my wife's return. You know, I would actually rather listen to suicidal patients for the rest of the afternoon than have to remain in my wife's shoes!"

I can't remember what words of wisdom transpired beyond that candid admission. The only thing that mattered was that another person was stumbling on the parenthood path like me—and a professional, no less, whom I assumed had all the answers!

I realized that this was no coincidental chance meeting via the air waves. God graciously showered me with encouragement and affirmation through the honest words of a struggling dad. In a desperate moment, my hand turned on the radio, but it was God, in His infinite wisdom, who orchestrated the timing.

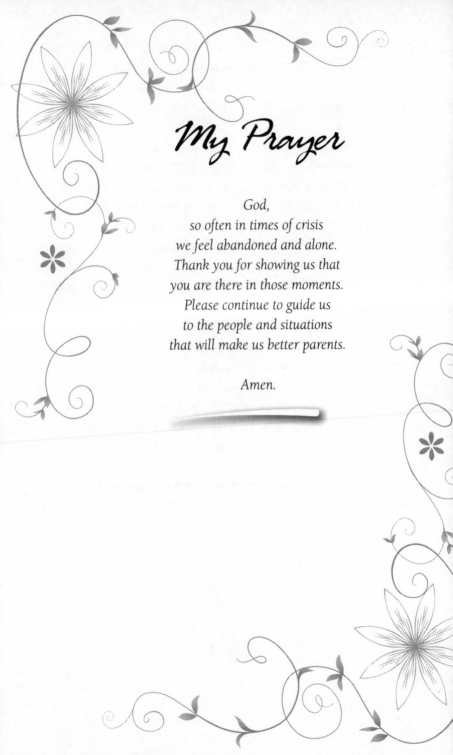

My Prayer

God,
so often in times of crisis
we feel abandoned and alone.
Thank you for showing us that
you are there in those moments.
Please continue to guide us
to the people and situations
that will make us better parents.

Amen.

52

The Doughnut Disaster

By Karen Talcott

*For the kingdom of God is not a matter of eating and drinking,
but of righteousness, peace and joy in the Holy Spirit
because anyone who serves Christ in this way
is pleasing to God and approved by men.*
~Romans 14:17-18

I promised my children that we were going to make home-made doughnuts one Saturday morning. I dusted off my Betty Crocker cookbook and found a recipe for cake doughnuts. Luckily, I had all the ingredients in our pantry and began the process in anticipation.

Now, anytime you try to cook with three young helpers, there is going to be some chaos involved. Things are going to spill, messes are going to be made, and some fairness issues will have to be worked out. It is during these moments that I realize I have some control issues.

I wanted this to be a wonderful bonding time with my children, as we filled the kitchen with the fragrant smells of cinnamon and sugar. But it soon became more about who had a turn mixing and pouring in the ingredients.

Then when it came time to cook the doughnuts, my children decided they were done and proceeded to watch TV. I cooked up the remaining doughnuts and then presented them with great flourish on a plate. Each child took one bite and then expressed that they didn't taste like Dunkin' Donuts. Their disappointment registered on their faces, and I felt let down from the whole experience.

It was my husband who came in to rescue the situation. He said to me, "Do not focus on the end result, but instead be happy with the time you spent with your children."

It was exactly what I needed to hear. I had made a memory with my children that morning in the kitchen. I had passed down tips in baking that I had learned from my own mother. God was there in that moment as He is there in all the moments, great and small. The experience changed in my mind, and I was able to see the humor and the love that were there all the time.

My Prayer

God,
how wonderful you are
to give us so many pleasures in this lifetime.
Help me each day to find humor
in situations that seem frustrating
and always remain in your loving service.

Amen.

"Just think... we're not just making doughnuts, we're making memories!"

53

The Cross by the Side of the Road

By Susan M. Heim

But let all who take refuge in you be glad;
let them ever sing for joy.
Spread your protection over them,
that those who love your name may rejoice in you.
For surely, O Lord, you bless the righteous;
you surround them with your favor as with a shield.
~Psalm 5:11-12

Every day when I drove my second-born son to middle school, I noticed a little wooden cross by the side of the road. The shoelaces on a worn pair of athletic shoes had been tied together and draped over the top of the cross. A weathered bouquet of plastic flowers lay at the base. It marked the site where a fourteen-year-old boy had been killed by a car as he crossed the street on his bicycle.

Tears would fill my eyes as I passed it because the boy was the same age as my oldest son. I couldn't help but think, "If it can happen to that child, it could happen to my own." I would think about how his family only had memories now of their beloved son and how their hearts must be aching.

My oldest son is now nineteen and in college, but I am still haunted by the boy on the bicycle. When my son is out late with his friends, I listen to storms raging outside and pray that he makes it home safely. Surely, the storm in my heart is just as fierce. I stay awake until I hear the door open and know that he is well. And I utter a prayer of thanksgiving that we both made it through the storm.

As the mother of four sons in a scary world, I know that I'll never completely stop worrying. But I know I need to try. When I worry so much about my children, I not only make myself miserable, but I hurt God with my lack of trust in Him. I want to pull my sons close and never let them out of my sight, but I know I can't protect them forever. I have to let go and let God be their protector.

My Prayer

God,
please extend your loving protection
to my children.
Help me to allow them their freedom
and to trust that you will care for them at all times.
For I know you are the ultimate parent,
dear Father, and you love my children
as much as I do.

Amen.

54

God's Perfect Timing

By Julie Cruz

Those who know your name will trust in you,
for you, LORD,
have never forsaken those who seek you.
~Psalm 9:10

My son had gone to a Christian school for seven years and was getting ready to go to a large public high school. I had gone to public school all my life, so I knew he wouldn't be getting all the "extras" he used to get, like chapel, prayer and religious class. Therefore, I wanted him to be able to attend a good youth group and invite his new friends to join him.

Unfortunately, our church's youth pastor had just moved, and we didn't have a strong youth group. We had been hoping and praying for one particular youth pastor to accept our church's call, but when he didn't, I thought, "This is terrible! Where will my son and his friends be able to get involved?"

I knew this was selfish, though, so I prayed to God and said, "I know that Kyle is yours, and I will trust you with him." I prayed that my need to control matters would be taken away, and I trusted that God would be there for Kyle and his needs.

When school started, I was so happy to learn that Kyle had met a new group of friends. They all came from a different Christian school, but they invited him to go to their youth group. Kyle loved it, and he now attends every week!

I was so happy that God provided for Kyle in His own way. I knew in time that we would get the right youth pastor, but it would be in God's timing. He knows the big picture and will provide when we give up our need for control. Not only did God provide for my son, but He also filled the need of our church and placed an amazing vicar to lead our youth group and congregation.

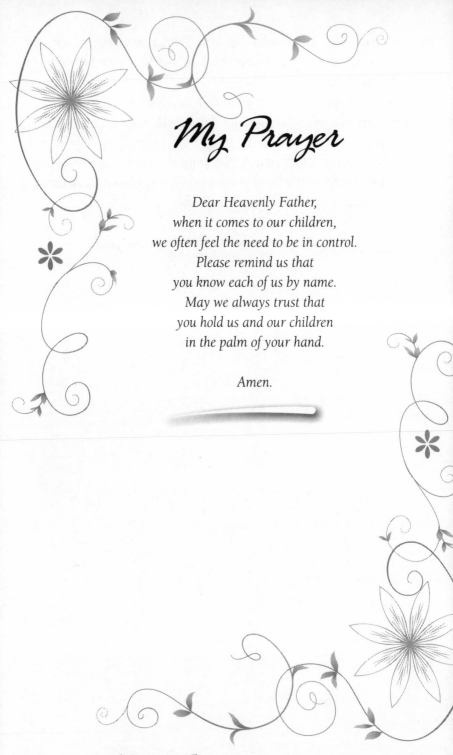

My Prayer

Dear Heavenly Father,
when it comes to our children,
we often feel the need to be in control.
Please remind us that
you know each of us by name.
May we always trust that
you hold us and our children
in the palm of your hand.

Amen.

55

Smacked with the Obvious

By Sandra Brese Rice

*Trust in the Lord with all your heart
and lean not on your own understanding;
in all your ways acknowledge Him,
and He will make your paths straight.*
~Proverbs 3:5-6

I don't think that I have ever had such a crazy first day of school with my children as I did the year my son moved to middle school. Two kids, two different schools, two different schedules for the day, two different buses and two different school districts... crazy!

Just when I thought I had the whole situation under control, life threw me a curveball. My son went from feeling really excited about attending his new school to complete deflation when his bus never came to get him.

After some quick thinking by my daughter's bus driver, my son got on her bus. I ran into the house and called the school, told them the story, and asked them to call me as soon as he arrived. Then, I waited and worried...

The thing is, I wasn't worried about his safety. I was worried about him worrying! I wished that I could tell him that he would be just fine. I wished that he knew I took care of the school and his teacher. I wished that he knew I had it all figured out when... BAM! *I was smacked with the obvious.*

We must frustrate God to no end! He loves us so much, and He would do anything for us. He knows our final destination and how to get us there safely. Why the lack of trust? Why the fear? I love when God gives me a good smack with the obvious. His reminders of His love, His strength, His power and even His existence are pretty awesome. Trust Him to be there for you... always.

My Prayer

Dear Lord,
thank you for loving me all the time,
even when I worry and am afraid.
Help me to lean on you in all things
and to trust that you are always there for me.
Thank you for the occasional reminders
of how much you love me.

Amen.

God Never Gives Up on Us

By Susan M. Heim

I write to you, dear children,
because your sins have been forgiven
on account of his name.
~1 John 2:12

My four-year-old twin sons were among eight preschoolers lined up on the pool wall for swimming class. Typical with a class of children that age, the kids were all goofing around—splashing each other, yelling, crying, and ignoring their instructor. The young teacher was becoming frustrated at having to repeat her directions over and over again.

One of the little girls jumped off the wall, where she'd been instructed to sit, and my son Caleb followed her into the water. The teacher lost her patience. "Sarah, Caleb, you're both done with class NOW!" She made them get out of the pool and go back to their mothers.

I reacted with anger. Why couldn't Caleb just follow directions and learn how to swim? And I was also upset with the teacher.

"We're paying good money for this class," I told myself. "Why doesn't this teacher realize that this behavior is age-appropriate and be more patient with these kids?"

Fortunately, at the next practice, Caleb was repentant, and the teacher was more tolerant of the kids' antics.

I realized that this situation was similar to the prodigal son. In the parable, even though the son squandered his inheritance on high living, the father welcomed him with open arms when he returned in shame. Aren't we fortunate that God never gives up on us, even when we ignore Him or sin against him time and time again? Unlike my son's swimming instructor, God has endless patience. He is a loving Father, willing to wait for our return. There is nothing He won't forgive if we repent, like the prodigal son.

My Prayer

Dear God,
thank you for being a
Father who never gives up on His children.
When we fail to listen
or wander far from you,
you patiently await us with open arms.
You never give up on us,
loving us unconditionally.
Help us to heed your call
to return to you when we are "lost."

Amen.

A Pat on the Back

By Lisa Murphy

God is not unjust;
He will not forget your work
and the love you have shown Him
as you have helped His people
and continue to help them.
~Hebrews 6:10

My children attend a wonderful Christian school where they are taught to truly have a heart for God and others. Every month, a child from each class is awarded a Christian Discipleship Award for being an example of Christian love.

Two years ago, my eight-year-old daughter, Meagan, had done a number of incredible things to help others. She gave all of her savings—a couple hundred dollars—to a little girl with terminal cancer in hope of a cure. She gave her hair to Locks of Love. She even gave her Christmas presents to a family that had very little. Yet, she never received the Christian Discipleship Award.

Every time the parent/teacher conferences would come around, she would mention the lack of recognition. I told her I could see that, as an eight-year-old, she would like something tangible, but that the best things she will ever do are only known by God. I would then ask if she wanted me to bring the matter to her teacher's attention, but she would always say "no."

On the last day of school, as we drove to the campus, again she mentioned the award. I told her that she was storing up wonderful treasures in heaven, and she seemed fine with that.

About ten minutes after the last day of school started, some students came to tell me that Meagan was going to be one of the two girls selected out of 500 students to receive the Star Award! This was an award given to the two students who demonstrated Christian love all year round. I was so grateful to God for giving my daughter a God-sized pat on the back.

My Prayer

Dear Lord,
please help me not to interfere
in the work you are doing in my children's lives.
So often I want to prevent them
from feeling disappointment.
Please help me to trust in you
because you are the perfect parent.

Amen.

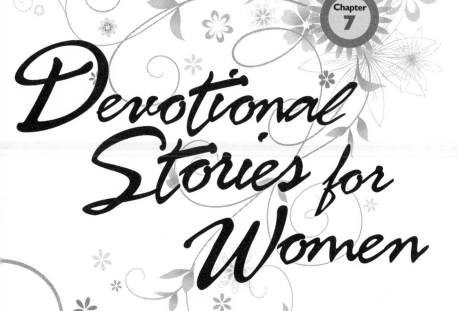

Devotional Stories for Women

Relationships

*May the Lord
make your love increase
and overflow for each other
and for everyone else.*

~1 Thessalonians 3:12

Chicken Soup
for the Soul

Appearances Can Be Deceiving

By Susan M. Heim

Therefore judge nothing before the appointed time;
wait till the Lord comes.
He will bring to light what is hidden in darkness
and will expose the motives of men's hearts.
At that time each will receive his praise from God.
~1 Corinthians 4:5

Miss Patrick. Just the mention of her name sent the teenagers in my high school running in terror. This tyrannical dictator was our English literature teacher. With the face of a bulldog and the temperament to match, she delighted in humiliation. Pity the teen who didn't have the assignment memorized—*and* recited in Old English. If the task wasn't done to her satisfaction, the slacker would be reduced to tears!

One afternoon, standing at my locker, I heard a sudden voice behind me: "I would like to speak with you."

My heart raced. I would know that voice anywhere! What had I done? I prayed Miss Patrick wouldn't humiliate me in front of everyone in the hallway.

"M-m-me?" I stammered. "You want to talk to me?"

She replied, "I heard you traveled to Japan last summer. I'm quite fond of travel myself and would like to hear about your trip."

She wanted to talk about *Japan*? I breathed a sigh of relief.

After taking a few moments to recover, something hit me with surprise: Miss Patrick's whole life didn't revolve around making us miserable! She was a real person with outside interests just like everyone else. It was a moment of clarity as I saw my teacher in a new light.

Later, we had a pleasant discussion. I never learned why Miss Patrick terrorized her students. Maybe she was toughening us up for the real world. Or, possibly, that was the only way she thought she could gain respect. But, even if we never learned to speak Old English, she taught me there's more depth to people than they show to the outside world. And, if you take time to get to know them, you might like them—at least a little bit!

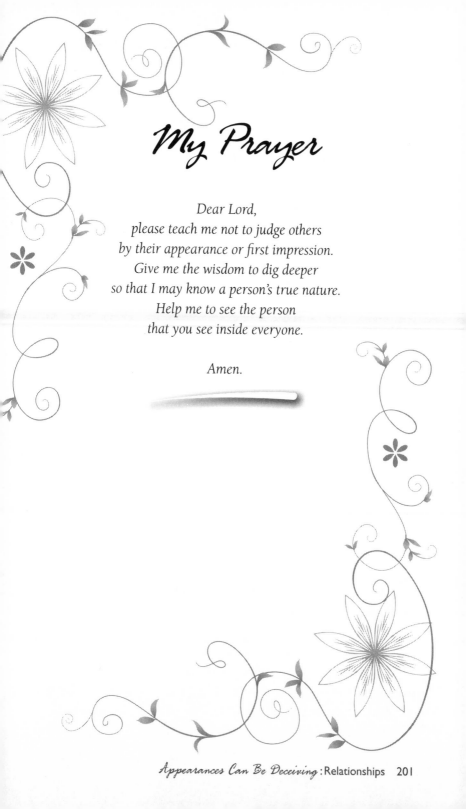

My Prayer

Dear Lord,
please teach me not to judge others
by their appearance or first impression.
Give me the wisdom to dig deeper
so that I may know a person's true nature.
Help me to see the person
that you see inside everyone.

Amen.

59

Chicken Soup for the Soul

Mending a Friendship

By Karen Talcott

Get rid of the old yeast
that you may be a new batch without yeast —
as you really are...
Therefore let us keep the Festival,
not with the old yeast, the yeast of malice and wickedness,
but with bread without yeast,
the bread of sincerity and truth.
~1 Corinthians 5:7-8

When I first moved to Florida, I felt so out of place. I had come from a small town out West and was so unsure of myself. Luckily, my husband and I moved into a friendly neighborhood, and things became instantly better.

For many years, my neighbor across the street and I shared happy times. But then a misunderstanding developed, and she quit speaking to me. I tried many times to speak to her about the issue and tell her how sorry I was that I had let her down. But she refused to take my phone calls and avoided me when I was outside.

During our stalemate, my husband and I put our house up for

sale. We weren't leaving the neighborhood out of spite; we were having twins and needed room for our growing family.

Months later, I moved away without talking to her and putting closure to our misunderstanding. It always left a raw place in my heart when I thought of how poorly it had ended. Many times in church when I prayed, I would flash back to this friendship. Sometimes, I would feel anger still lurking in my heart. Other times, I wanted to find peace again. I just hated the feelings left from our unresolved dispute. It was like a scab that kept reopening and festering with pain and frustration.

About eight months after we moved, I decided to take a drive back into the old neighborhood. As I drove down my street, I saw my former neighbor out in her front yard washing her car. I knew that I needed to stop and greet her. I opened up the car door and got out. To my surprise, she came up and gave me a big hug. We both apologized for our actions, and I felt that closure had finally occurred. I was able to say I was sorry and have it accepted. I know that God heard my prayers and arranged for us to meet that day.

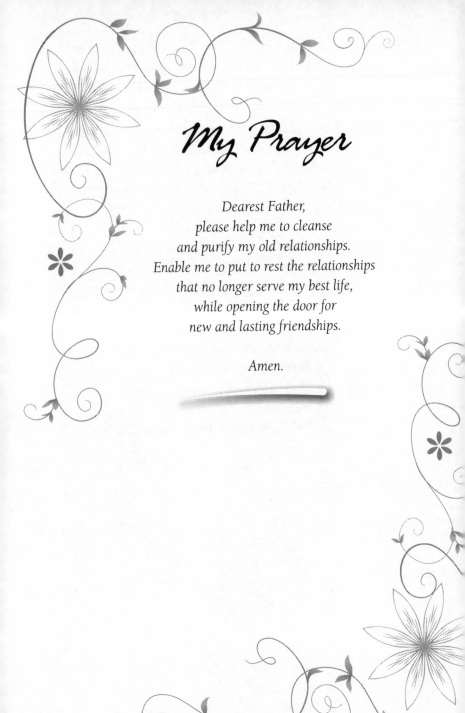

My Prayer

Dearest Father,
please help me to cleanse
and purify my old relationships.
Enable me to put to rest the relationships
that no longer serve my best life,
while opening the door for
new and lasting friendships.

Amen.

60

Clearing Away the Clutter

By Susan M. Heim

You shall not make for yourself an idol
in the form of anything in heaven above
or on the earth beneath or in the waters below.
~Exodus 20:4

"Why do you want to save all these books?" my husband asked recently as we were trying to condense some of the items we had stored in the garage.

Books are like friends to me. If I've read a book that I dearly love, I can't bear to get rid of it. But my husband sees them as unnecessary clutter.

"Well, what about all this stuff *you* have in the garage?" I countered.

Every tool known to mankind, partial cans of paint, and assorted containers of hardware had all been saved in the unlikely possibility that we might need them for some future home project. But to my husband, these things were much more useful than a bunch of old books.

Experts say that too much clutter can actually add stress to our lives. And I can attest that *fighting* about clutter isn't very relaxing either. The Bible points out that the accumulation of things means that we place a high value on our possessions—sort of like worshipping false idols. When we become too attached to the "things" in our lives, they come to mean more to us than anything else—even God.

I asked God to help me whittle down my book collection. I allocated some to donate to the library while putting others aside to sell on the Internet. I realized that I hadn't looked at these books in years, and it was highly unlikely that I ever would. They were just clutter, plain and simple.

From then on, I would do my best to make my relationship with God my most precious possession. What kind of clutter is standing between you and God?

My Prayer

God,
please help me to eliminate
the unnecessary clutter in my life.
Enable me to see that my possessions
are just "things"
and not objects of worship.
May I always consider my faith
and my relationships to be the best—
and most important—
things I own.

Amen.

" I think a higher power just made the decluttering decision for us!"

61

My Grandmother's Lesson

By Tracy Powell

Your beauty should not come from
outward adornment, such as braided hair
and the wearing of gold jewelry and fine clothes.
Instead, it should be that of your inner self,
the unfading beauty of a gentle and quiet spirit,
which is of great worth in God's sight.
~1 Peter 3:3-4

few years after my grandmother passed away, my grandfather let me dig through their old photos. I came across a picture that fascinated me. My beautiful grandmother was dressed impeccably, beaming with joy against the backdrop of the ocean. I showed the photo to my grandfather, and a smile spread across his face. His green eyes lit up as he took the photo in his shaky hands and looked at his "Anna."

He told me how my grandmother had been left destitute when my biological grandfather had left her. Her children, including my mother, were very young. My grandmother was forced to move back in with her parents and support her family with hardly any income.

But through all the hardship, she never got depressed. When things would go from bad to worse, she would call her girlfriends, get dolled up, and go to the ocean for the day. Things eventually turned around, and she remarried. My grandfather helped raise her children.

That night in bed at my grandfather's house, I admired this photo for hours under the dim bedside lamp. I considered what it must have been like for her when her husband went to the grocery store one day and never returned. I thought about how unwanted she must have felt, how lonely and scared she must have been. But in that photo, I saw none of those feelings. I only saw a gorgeous woman entirely enjoying herself and the wonderful beauty around her that the Lord had blessed her with.

I brought the photo home with me, and I keep it at my desk while I pursue my own dreams. When things start to get rough, I see my grandmother saying to me as she stands next to the ocean, "Go call your girls, get dolled up, and enjoy God's gift to you... life!" I obey her voice and call on my friends, with whom I find warmth and support.

Like my grandmother, I bond with nature and remember I am a creation of God. It reminds me of my gifts and why I am here. When I return to my desk, I am invigorated, ready to tackle my destiny once again.

My Prayer

Dear Father,
thank you for bringing people into our lives
who inspire us to pursue our dreams
amid not-so-perfect circumstances.
Help me to remember the beautiful woman I am,
the lovely friends I have,
and the wonders of nature that enlighten my soul.
These things remind me that
you have given us a tremendous gift —
life!

Amen.

In Memory of Anna Marie McKenzie Cinpinski

62

Chicken Soup
for the *Soul*

Do What's Right

By Cindy Dumke

Then the LORD said to Cain,
"Why are you angry? Why is your face downcast?
If you do what is right, will you not be accepted?
But if you do not do what is right,
sin is crouching at your door;
it desires to have you,
but you must master it."
~Genesis 4:6-8

My teenage son had been working on a science fair project that involved electrical circuits and using a potato as the power source. According to theory, a potato can generate enough power to light a small flashlight bulb. We had purchased several small flashlight bulbs, but he was unable to get any of them to light.

One day after school, we stopped at a local store to purchase incidental household items. As we walked past the decorative lighting department, I saw boxes of strings of lights and thought that perhaps a potato could light this kind of bulb.

I thought to myself, "I don't need a whole string. I'll just 'borrow' one of the lights in the string so my son can test it to see if it works. I'll return it later that evening."

I discreetly plucked one of the bulbs and concealed it in my hand. When I looked at my son's face, I could see that what I was doing made him very uncomfortable.

I said to him, "You don't think I should do this, do you?"

He immediately responded, "No. What if someone buys that string of lights?"

I put the bulb back in the string of lights. When we got back to the car, I put my hand on his shoulder and said, "Thank you for helping me do the right thing."

He looked at me and said, "I learned it from you, Mom."

I realized then that I need to be a good Christian role model all of the time because my kids are always watching and learning from me. My son could have made me feel shame. Instead, he showed me mercy and love, just like our Heavenly Father does every day.

My Prayer

Dear Father,
sometimes it is so convenient
to take the easy way out.
We want to finish our commitments
and through our rushing,
we don't make the best decisions.
I pray today that I remember
I am an example to all those around me.
Let me shine with your love
and reflect only what is pleasing in your eyes.

Amen.

"Even if I don't win the Science Fair, doing the right thing makes us winners in life!"

63

Hope for the Prodigal

By L.M.

So he got up and went to his father.
But while he was still a long way off,
his father saw him and
was filled with compassion for him;
he ran to his son, threw his arms around him
and kissed him.
~Luke 15:20

It had been twenty-seven years since I'd seen or spoken to my big brother. When I was seventeen and he was twenty-two, he started "finding himself" through drugs and bad company. I was finding myself through Christ. I went to college, got a job, got married, had kids, loved the Lord, and prayed for my brother.

My mom and dad also prayed for my brother. Every now and then, we'd talk about him, and they would tell me how much they loved him.

One day, I dropped my daughter off at dance class and started thinking about my brother on the drive home. I realized that while I had prayed for my brother to find the saving and healing power of Christ, I'd never really forgiven him for the awful stuff he had brought into my life when I was seventeen. I made the decision to forgive my brother, and then I asked God to find a way to let him know.

The very next day, he called our father's house. It must have been a hard day for him because he found out from my stepmother that both Mom and Dad had died. My stepmother took his phone numbers without giving him mine, and we passed the information about his phone call along the family grapevine.

When I finally summoned the courage to call my brother, he was on his way to the hospital for minor surgery. I was able to tell him how much Mom and Dad had loved him, and I granted him my forgiveness, too. He went into surgery with a peaceful heart. I knew that God had orchestrated that phone call when my brother needed it most.

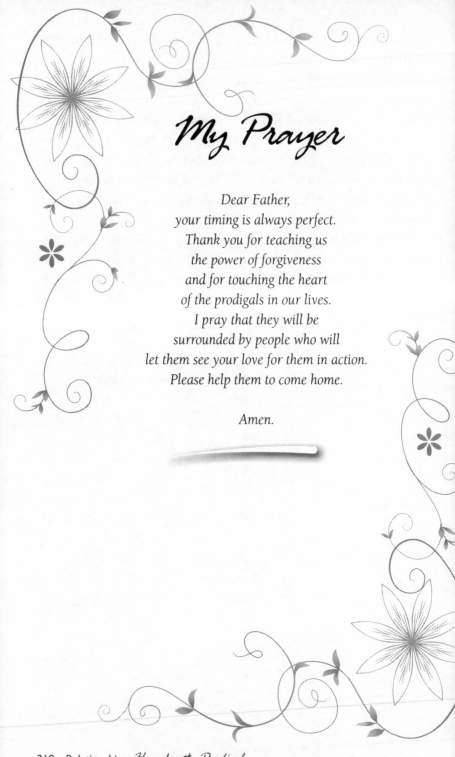

My Prayer

Dear Father,
your timing is always perfect.
Thank you for teaching us
the power of forgiveness
and for touching the heart
of the prodigals in our lives.
I pray that they will be
surrounded by people who will
let them see your love for them in action.
Please help them to come home.

Amen.

64

Conflict with a Co-Worker

By Karen Talcott

But the meek will inherit the land and enjoy great peace.
~Psalm 37:11

The morning started out fine, and I quickly organized my to-do list at work. But when my co-worker came in, she immediately had an issue she wanted to discuss. It was about her hours and the changes she wanted to make. Unfortunately, those changes were not conducive to my schedule. This created an instant conflict and was a sticking point in our interactions from that moment on. She felt strongly about her position, and I was irritated that she wanted to change the schedule that had always worked.

For the next few hours, we both proceeded to utilize the passive-aggressive approach, ignoring the other person and continuing with our work. Was it the best and most grown-up method to use? Of course not! But it is one I have a tendency to revert to in these types of situations.

As I picked up lunch that day, I made it a point to listen to Christian music in the car. I sang at the top of my lungs about Jesus' great love for us and His power of forgiveness. I also prayed that God would heal the situation for both my co-worker and me.

Did we resolve our conflict that day? I have to say the answer was no. But was there a softening on both our parts and some laughter by the end of the day? Yes, and I give God all the credit for starting to heal our work relationship again. God didn't "solve" the problem immediately, but He did open the door for love and compassion to come through. And, with love, anything is possible!

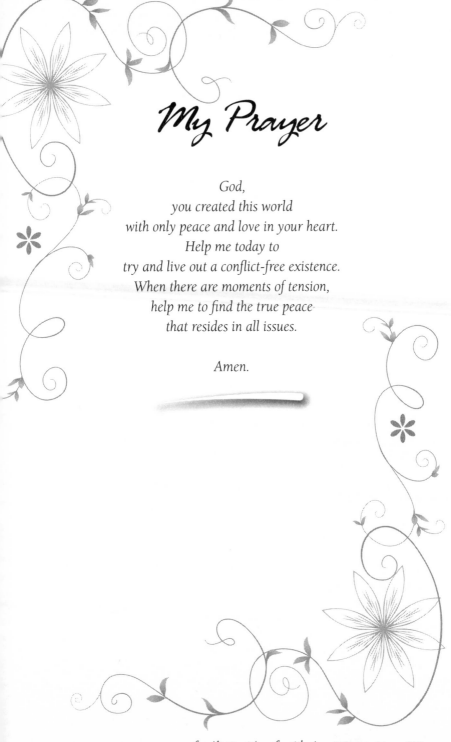

My Prayer

God,
you created this world
with only peace and love in your heart.
Help me today to
try and live out a conflict-free existence.
When there are moments of tension,
help me to find the true peace
that resides in all issues.

Amen.

65

Loose Lips

By Susan M. Heim

*A fool finds no pleasure in understanding
but delights in airing his own opinions.*
~Proverbs 18:2

One day at the grocery store, I was telling a woman I had just met about my twin sons, Caleb and Austen. She complimented me on the boys' names.

"Oh, thanks," I replied. "Don't you just hate it when people give their twins sound-alike names like Brandon and Brandi or Marlene and Darlene?"

I was puzzled when the woman merely replied with a weak smile and abruptly headed over to the produce section.

A few months later, to my surprise, I ran into the same woman again at a Moms of Multiples meeting. Everyone around the table took turns telling about their families.

"I have twin baby boys," this woman told the group. "Their names are 'Jimmy' and 'Jamie.'"

I wanted to crawl under the table in the hope that she wouldn't see me!

Another time I was talking about kitchens with a woman from work.

"I don't know why people are stupid enough to choose white cabinets," I blurted out. "They show every fingerprint!"

A few weeks later, this woman had the "girls" from the office over for a party. Her teenage daughter took me on a tour of the house.

"Mom just redid the kitchen a month ago," she explained. "She put in all new countertops and cabinets." Guess what color they were...

Even though I never meant to be mean-spirited, I nonetheless managed to insult these two women with my "loose lips." If, like me, you are a member of the "open mouth, insert foot club," remind yourself that God gave us the gift of gab to do good and spread his word, not to judge others' choices or criticize those who do things differently from us. God doesn't judge the color of our cupboards or the names we give our children—and neither should we.

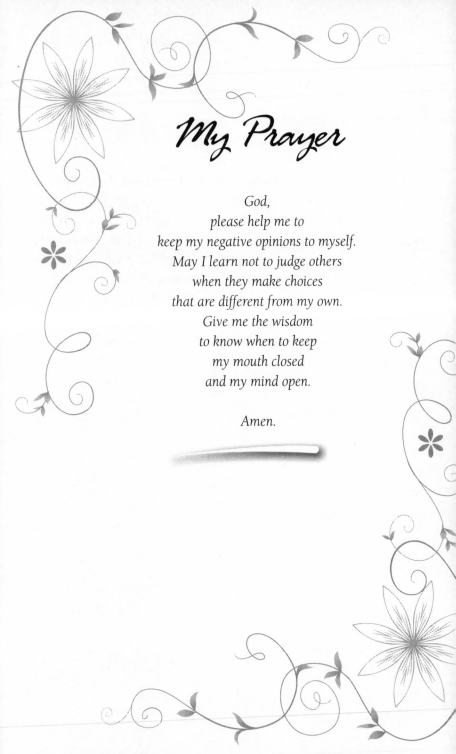

My Prayer

God,
please help me to
keep my negative opinions to myself.
May I learn not to judge others
when they make choices
that are different from my own.
Give me the wisdom
to know when to keep
my mouth closed
and my mind open.

Amen.

"I'm so sorry I made fun of your boys' names. I have a funny name, too. Just call me Ms. Foot in Mouth!"

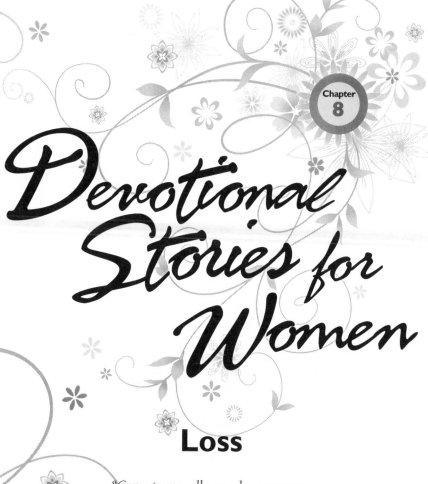

Devotional Stories for Women

Loss

*"Come to me, all you who are weary
and burdened, and I will give you rest.
Take my yoke upon you and learn from me,
for I am gentle and humble in heart,
and you will find rest for your souls.
For my yoke is easy and my burden is light."*

~Matthew 11:28-30

Words to Live By

By Christina M. Harris

Therefore do not worry about tomorrow,
for tomorrow will worry about itself.
Each day has enough trouble of its own.
~Matthew 6:34

The sun beamed in through the big bay window and masked the dank and dark feeling that only a hospital room can provide. A line of light illuminated my grandfather's face, and for just a moment he closed his eyes as if allowing the warmth of the sun to saturate his entire body. When your life is approaching its end, I imagine all the bitterness subsides, and the jaded moments that we put so much stock in become petty and meaningless.

My grandfather opened his eyes slowly and said, "Don't live your life without living it. I worked too hard. I missed many things because I was trying to make a better tomorrow for my family. What good is a tomorrow if you keep missing today?"

He rolled back over and closed his eyes once more as if allowing what he said to marinate within me. I realized, with the sun basking on his pale and aged face and his eyes closed in deep contemplation, that he was reviewing his life as if he were a bystander. I knew that when my grandfather spoke those words to me, he was feeling regret. Though we cannot change the past, we can influence the future.

I was twenty-two years old—an unstoppable college graduate with the sky as my limit. I knew that my grandfather was bestowing upon me yet another valuable tool to add to my defense against this sometimes harsh world.

That night, I slept the soundest I ever had. A sense of peace and tranquility fell over me that I hadn't felt in a long while. My worries, cares and concerns seemed weightless and were replaced by the almost haunting sound of my grandfather. "Don't live your life without living it."

I was abruptly woken out of a sound sleep by my mother. Before she muttered the words through sobs and tears, I knew why she was waking me.

Later that morning as I sat at the kitchen table, a single tear ran down my face. Through the window, a ray of sunlight engulfed my entire body and warmed me from the inside out. I knew it was a hug from my grandfather. And I knew that for the rest of my life his words would reverberate in my thoughts. He had given me the best advice I ever had.

My Prayer

Lord,
how we lead our life
is a gift to you.
Our time here on Earth
can be short, long, fulfilling,
or full of pain and suffering.
Remind us each day to live it for you.
When we center it on you,
all things are possible.

Amen.

Losing a Child

By Nancy Purcell

Whatever is true, whatever is noble, whatever is right, whatever is pure, whatever is lovely, whatever is admirable, if anything is excellent or praiseworthy — think about such things.
~Philippians 4:8

There are times when our faith is tested to the maximum. The death of my sixteen-year-old daughter was by far the biggest test I've ever undergone.

I was divorced and alone in my home when that phone call came: *Are you Cathy's mother? Is anyone there with you? I have bad news.* Although my house was empty, I was not alone. An inner strength seemed to have literally gripped me and held me fast, even as I spit out doubts and screamed at the minister on the other end of the line, even as I ran from room to room begging God to let this be some mistake.

Then a calm—yes, a calm—momentarily rested on me, and I called a friend for help. Within an hour, my house was filled with adults and teenagers, all crying and asking in disbelief, "Why?" Ah, the "why" thing. Who knows why? The answers to such questions are only revealed to us in His time.

As He carried me across my barren wasteland, I thought on

my daughter's purity, her loveliness, the admiration that a host of young people eloquently expressed to me through the months that followed.

Twenty-five years later, I still think on her truth, her love of Christ, and her joyfulness as I dig in the earth and plant seeds, expecting a garden of beauties to rise come spring. And they do, just as Christ did that Easter morning. Because of Him, I never think of her as lost; I know where she is.

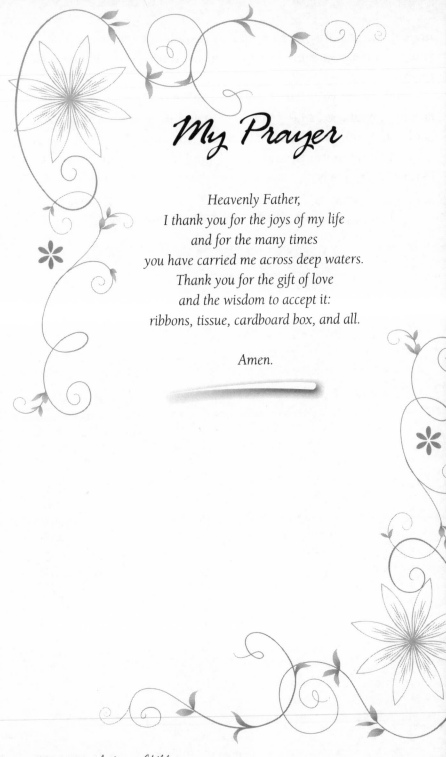

My Prayer

Heavenly Father,
I thank you for the joys of my life
and for the many times
you have carried me across deep waters.
Thank you for the gift of love
and the wisdom to accept it:
ribbons, tissue, cardboard box, and all.

Amen.

68

The "Gucci" Bag

By Loretta D. Schoen

Therefore we do not lose heart.
Though outwardly we are wasting away,
yet inwardly we are being renewed day by day.
For our light and momentary troubles
are achieving for us an eternal glory
that far outweighs them all.
~2 Corinthians 4:16-17

t was a serious and solemn time for us—the end of my mother's life on Earth. She had tried every drug and therapy known at the time to kill or stave off the cancer, to no avail. As it ravaged her body, she became unable to walk, even with the assistance of a walker. She had been such a fighter, but now she was telling us she was ready to leave this Earth, and that God was waiting for her. She stated that she didn't care what we did with her "stuff." She made some suggestions and said she wanted to go "home." She had no regrets with her life.

So, we began what can only be called a "death watch." We soon settled into a schedule whereby my brothers and husband took turns staying with her at night, and my mother-in-law (a nurse) and I stayed with her during the day. Movement was excruciating, and so repositioning was done only to reduce the bed sores, and a morphine drip was given for the increasing pain. Going to the bathroom became an exhausting and painful chore, so she was catheterized.

Mom began to separate herself from her earthly life, speaking less and less. She began dreaming or talking to people who had passed on before her. When she did speak, it was in short sentences or words. On one such occasion, she woke up and began pulling on her catheter tube, trying to pull it out. The chemo nurse, Linda, now a friend of my mother's, was staying on to assist us in her hospice care.

Linda took my mother's hand and said, "Gloria, leave that alone. It's your 'Gucci' bag."

My mom opened her eyes and looked down at the bag, and then straight into Linda's eyes and said, "Well, darling, if that's my 'Gucci' bag, then it better match my outfit because God's waiting for me!"

My mother was dying just as she had lived: embracing life and death with faith, love, and a sense of humor!

My Prayer

Dear Lord,
help me to remember that
this life is a stepping stone to eternal life with you.
Earthly things can't compare to the
riches that await us in heaven.
May we learn to let go of the need
to accumulate "stuff" on our earthly journey
and to value those things—
like love, faith and a sense of humor!—
that we can carry with us
when we come "home" to you.

Amen.

"Look at that! My Gucci bag goes well with my wings!"

The Times of Our Lives

By Audrey Valeriani

Joy is gone from our hearts;
our dancing has turned to mourning.
~Lamentations 5:15

During my ninth week-long trip to Aruba with my husband, we spent our time relaxing under a tree and swimming at the beach during the day, and then sharing exquisite dinners and romantic walks in the evenings. We didn't take any photos because we had visited the island many times before and already had plenty of pictures. On our way to the airport we joked that, other than our tanned skin, we had no proof that we had traveled there!

As we stood in line at check-in, we noticed a family who had been on our chartered plane ride down the week before. This day, however, they all had swollen and tear-filled eyes. Sniffling, they shared only an occasional whispered comment. On the plane, we sat directly behind them: a mother and her four children, ages 8 to 16, with no dad in attendance. We learned that the father had been killed in a jet-skiing accident that week, and his wife and children had to bravely make their way home without him.

We watched the moods of the children go from seemingly care-free while playing cards to quiet sobbing when idle, but the mother's face was chilling. Between hopping seats in an effort to attend to her devastated children, she would sit and stare down at her lap, unable to comprehend what had happened. We could almost feel her pain as we realized that this could have happened to any of us that week. While we were laughing and playing in the water, eating chocolate desserts to our heart's content, this poor family had been experiencing the tragedy of their lives. The vacation they had dreamed about had turned into a nightmare they would never forget. Their photographs would capture indelible moments that would haunt them forever.

I suddenly regretted that we had no pictures from this vacation together. I wondered if the memorialization of events in our minds is only triggered by traumatic events. I closed my eyes and scanned my memory, hoping that my mind had properly registered all the wonderful moments I had shared with my husband that week.

Throughout our lives, our hearts will begin to show the wear and tear from the inevitable misfortunes that befall us. We must consciously stop time and record with our minds those moments that make our hearts swell with love and gratitude—the intimate moments, the surprises, the hours spent with loved ones and friends... *all* the times of our lives.

My Prayer

Dear Father,
please help us to remember
to cherish the good times of our lives,
lest we forget them in the midst of
the storms that will surely come.
We know that you are with us
in times of sorrow and joy.
May we see the beauty
in the moments we spend
with our families and loved ones.

Amen.

Midnight Message

By Carol Holmes

As a mother comforts her child, so will I comfort you.
~Isaiah 66:13

In August of 2002, my mother went to the hospital for surgery. The doctor said everything went well with the procedure.

The next day, I went to visit her and was told that she was doing so well that she would probably be coming home the next day. Not even one hour later, after I had just finished brushing her hair (she always loved that), she died in my arms. A blood clot had traveled from her leg to her heart.

I was crushed and broken. The day before the surgery, she had told me she was nervous, but if anything happened, she knew that God would be taking her to heaven. I just couldn't believe how things could change so quickly.

That night, I went to bed, but I awoke crying after midnight. I turned on the TV (which is something that I never do in the middle of the night), and there on the TV screen was a beautiful scene.

I saw trees and flowers and a brook. A beautiful song was playing, and on the screen were these words, "As a mother comforts her child, so will I comfort you" (Isaiah 66:13). God is so good.

My Prayer

Dear Father,
you always know what we need
and when we need it.
Thank you for being ever-present
in our daily lives,
ready to provide the comfort we so desire.
We are so fortunate to be children of God,
loved by a Father
who takes care of our every need.

Amen.

A Friend's Eternal Love

By Cathy Carpinello

A friend loves at all times.
~Proverbs 17:17

"Cathy, you have to come to the hospital to say good-bye to Jodi."

Those words still echo in my head two years after the death of my oldest and dearest friend. She had suffered a brain aneurysm that morning while blow-drying her hair as she did every morning before going to work. It was a typical morning by all accounts. I walked into that intensive-care room to see her family huddled around the bed in shock.

"Jodi Lynn," I said, "it's me, Cathy. I know you can hear me."

The nurses said the last sense to go is hearing, so with only the Holy Spirit to guide me, I prayed as I had never prayed before. Her body began to twitch, and it was obvious to all that God had allowed her to hear my prayer. The entire room was stunned at the power and presence that filled the room. The Holy Spirit was there; I had nothing to do with it.

Jodi hadn't established a relationship with God yet, and this wasn't the first time I had prayed for her. Unfortunately, it would be the last. When I gave my life to Jesus Christ many years before, she thought I was crazy. We had lived quite the party life as young girls, and she couldn't understand the way God had changed me. As we aged, it made her uncomfortable, but we still remained best friends. Jodi was as unselfish as you can be without knowing the Lord, and in her death she demonstrated that. As a transplant donor, she saved many lives that night.

I think often about what she might have said to God when she stood before Him. Did I pray hard enough for her all those years? Did she hear me that night on her deathbed and finally say "yes" to Jesus? Oh, how I pray that is what happened. But I know that our God is just and fair. And I find great comfort in the fact that I was able to be with Jodi in the final hours. I know that God put me beside her bed to pray for her. Whatever her decision, God used me in His service that night for Jodi and her family.

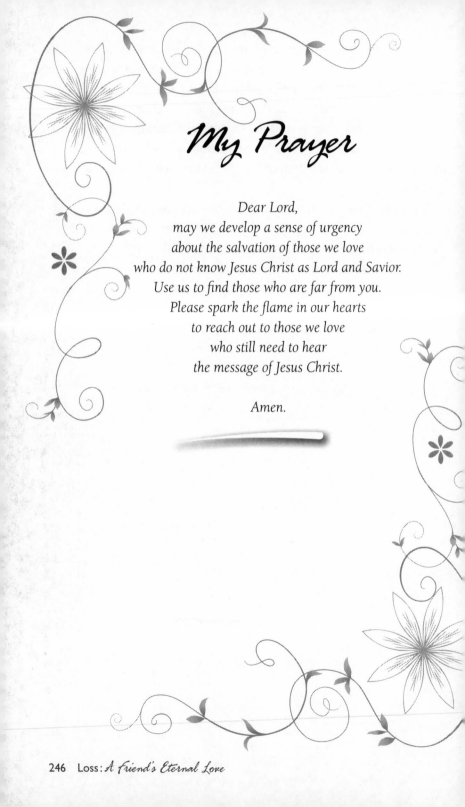

My Prayer

Dear Lord,
may we develop a sense of urgency
about the salvation of those we love
who do not know Jesus Christ as Lord and Savior.
Use us to find those who are far from you.
Please spark the flame in our hearts
to reach out to those we love
who still need to hear
the message of Jesus Christ.

Amen.

May the Lord Give You Peace

By Catherine Berg

Now may the Lord of peace himself
give you peace at all times and in every way.
The Lord be with all of you.
~2 Thessalonians 3:16

Nine months before my mother's death, I was shot in the chest at close range. The bullet traveled through my right arm, sliced my right lung, punctured the right atrium of my heart, and left my body through my rib cage. The gunshot wound resulted in the loss of my right lung, and led to herniated discs, arthritis, and sleep apnea. But, more importantly, it brought my six siblings together to help me through my troubled times.

At the age of twenty-seven, I believed that they, along with our dear mother, would always be by my side to hold my hand. But I was wrong.

On a chilly August day, at a memorial service for my mother, my brother Walt revealed to me that I was holding our mother's silver cross. Walt said that when I was in a coma in the hospital after the shooting, she had placed it in my hand. And on the evening of her death, I had placed that same cross in her hands, which she had held to her heart while grasping for her very last breath. The silver cross hung over my mother's beatless heart.

I always knew that following the way of the cross would heal my wounded heart. And that my knees would not scar from kneeling with folded hands in front of my dying mother in the coldest August I had ever felt on my fingertips. I thank God each and every day that I have one more day to do His work, to help others believe. To this day, eight years later, my mother's silver cross still brings warmth to my heart.

My Prayer

Heavenly Father,
please heal us from the inside out,
and also from the outside in.
May we find rest...
and peace...
in you.

Amen.

73

Learning to Love Again

By Karen Talcott

And God said,
"Let the land produce living creatures according to their kinds:
livestock, creatures that move along the ground,
and wild animals, each according to its kind."
And it was so.
~Genesis 1:24

We had Noah, our beloved Collie, for thirteen years. He had the most gentle spirit and loving way about him. He finally died after cancer invaded his beautiful body. We grieved as a family and felt such a loss in our house without his presence. Our household was missing something, and we all knew what it was.

For us, a family pet played an integral part in our house. I missed the evening walks with him around the neighborhood. He never pulled, yanked, or misbehaved on the leash. People had commented for years about his gentle demeanor and the way he pranced when walking. He could have been a show dog, but we never went that route. He was just part of our family.

We mourned his passing for quite a while, but God had something else in store for us. There were so many animals without homes, needing the love and attention that we could give them. God knew that by giving love again, we would fill the sadness in our hearts. Saying my prayers one night, I asked God to help us find the right pet to fill our house. We had been so lucky with Noah. Could we be blessed again?

My husband had been visiting the local animal shelter every now and then to see if a Collie came in. One day, he came home and talked about these two Golden Retrievers. They were sisters who had been brought to the shelter when their owner died. I knew that Golden Retrievers were a gentle breed and especially fond of children. Two dogs seemed like a lot to handle, but we knew what God had in store for us.

My husband brought home the dogs the next day. These two dogs are truly gifts to our family. They are extremely sweet and house-trained, and were waiting to be loved. By rescuing them, we found our "home" again.

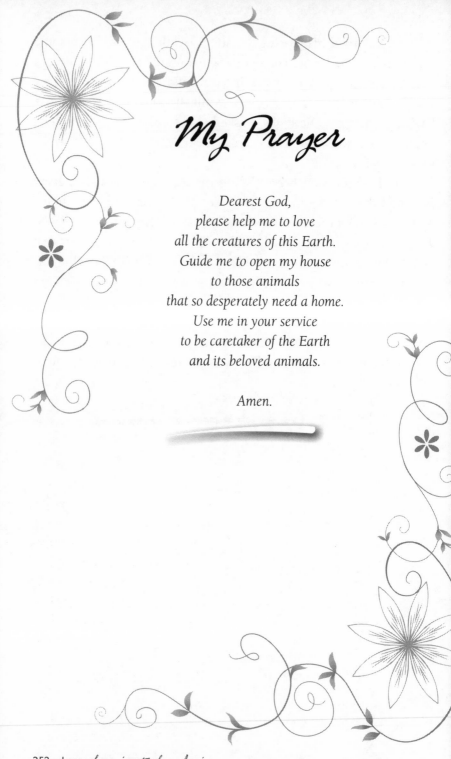

My Prayer

Dearest God,
please help me to love
all the creatures of this Earth.
Guide me to open my house
to those animals
that so desperately need a home.
Use me in your service
to be caretaker of the Earth
and its beloved animals.

Amen.

74

Hands Stretched Out

By Janice Flood Nichols

Jesus called out with a loud voice,
"Father, into your hands I commit my spirit."
~Luke 23:46

Mom had suffered a massive stroke. Unable to be rehabilitated, our family opted to take her home rather than move her to a long-term facility. It had always been her wish to die in her own surroundings, provided only with comfort care.

Her last few days on Earth were characterized by what we came to describe as her "party." Mom seemed to be suspended somewhere between this world and the next. Though she appeared unaware of her earthly caregivers, she seemed fixated on "people" or "things" that occupied space at ceiling level in the room we had converted to accommodate her needs. She would wink and exclaim with expressions that were distinctly hers, though she had long ceased communicating with her earthly family. What was going on? What was she seeing? Who was she seeing? Clearly, not strangers.

As I watched my mother transition from this life to the next, I came to believe that God, in His infinite love and mercy, had granted our family a glimpse into life's most poignant and final journey—a journey that may well be guided by those who have already crossed over. We were privy to a peaceful, glorious transformation. While her loved ones on this side whispered that it was okay to let go, perhaps her loved ones on the other side (Dad, my twin brother Frankie, grandparents, aunts, and uncles) were whispering, "Be patient, Dorothy. We will help you. Take our hands. The angels are here to carry you home."

It has been many years since I witnessed Mom's final days—days that give testimony to the fact that something miraculous takes place as we travel from this life to the next. I will be forever grateful for the gift of Mom's "party." We are never alone, even when our Earth eyes prevent us from seeing the light and love that await us all.

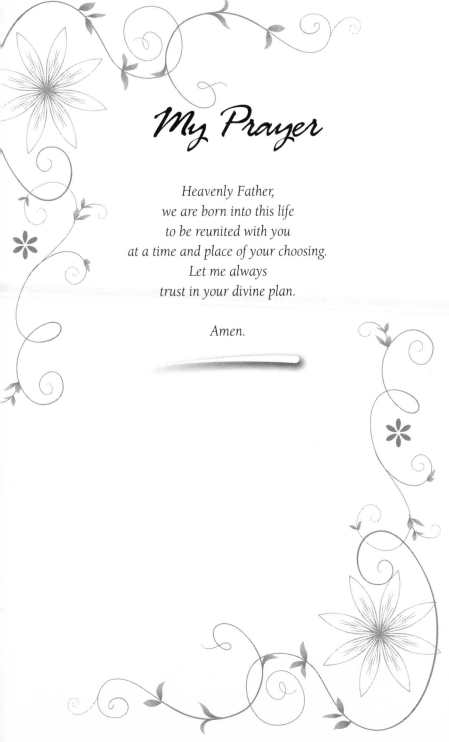

My Prayer

Heavenly Father,
we are born into this life
to be reunited with you
at a time and place of your choosing.
Let me always
trust in your divine plan.

Amen.

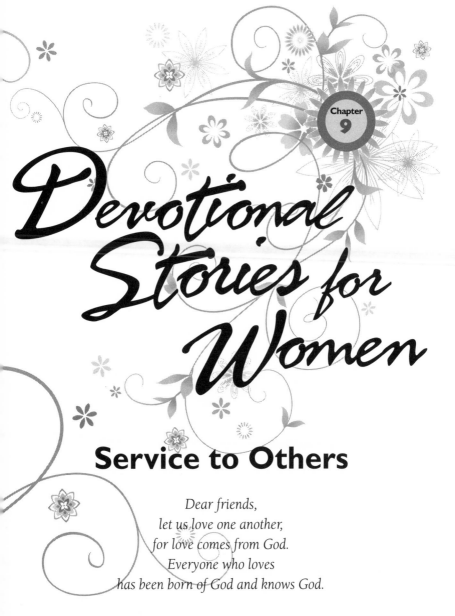

Devotional Stories for Women

Service to Others

*Dear friends,
let us love one another,
for love comes from God.
Everyone who loves
has been born of God and knows God.*

~1 John 4:7

Waiting for Jesus

By Carrie Ellis

But, if we walk in the light,
as he is in the light,
we have fellowship with one another.
~1 John 1:7

had seen her there many times, standing by the side of the road in her Sunday best. Each time I saw her, I thought to myself, "She must be waiting for the bus to attend church." I marveled at her dedication to whatever she was doing. Something drew me to her, but something else held me back from getting to know her.

I almost never go to Winn-Dixie in my area as it is not in the best part of town, but on this day I was looking for powdered sugar, and my usual store had none. I was desperate to find some for a project I had to complete.

"Perhaps Winn-Dixie carries it," I thought. "I'll just swing in and see."

There she was standing outside Winn-Dixie in her Sunday best. I walked up to the door, and she proudly announced, "Jesus loves you!"

I smiled and said, "Yes, I know, and I am so glad He does!"

To which she gave a resounding, "Praise the Lord Jesus!"

In the store, I wondered how this woman was going to get home. On the way out, I told her, "I live in your neighborhood, and I see you standing by the road waiting for the bus. Can I give you a ride?"

"I don't take the bus," she replied. "My Jesus sends a ride for me."

I pressed on. "Well, can I give you a ride today?"

She responded, "Oh, no, I can't go now. I must stay here and tell people about Jesus."

I wasn't about to give up. "I have another errand to run and will be coming back by here in about thirty minutes. Can I swing in and pick you up?"

In her thick Haitian accent, she said, "Oh, no, I must work for the Lord. I won't go home until around 9:00."

I was certainly confounded by this situation. I went on to my errand and went home, but my neighbor's faith and commitment to the Lord tugged at my heart. I felt the Lord telling me to go and pick her up. It wasn't convenient. It wasn't in the best part of town. But the Lord was doing something here, and I chose to obey.

As I pulled into the Winn-Dixie parking lot at 8:45, her face lit up. I think she was surprised to see me. I got out of my car, opened the door for her and said, "Jesus sent me to give you a ride."

A few people were standing around, and I wondered what they were thinking when they saw this middle-class white lady coming to pick up an elderly black Haitian woman in a bad part of town, announcing that Jesus had sent her. The Lord was delivering several messages that evening to a variety of people if they were willing to listen. But for me the message was loud and clear: Put God first, and He will take care of the rest.

My Prayer

Lord,
in all your infinite ways,
I thank you for using me in your service.
Just as Jesus taught us
that action speaks louder than words,
today I, too,
learned this valuable lesson.

Amen.

Are You Listening?

By Kim Leonard

In the same way,
let your light shine before men,
that they see your good deeds
and praise your Father in heaven.
~Matthew 5:16

Five days a week, I received radiation treatment for breast cancer. While sitting in the waiting room, I often found myself observing other people, trying to figure out their story. I couldn't help thinking how strange it was that I was among these people. I was a young mom with three little girls. How on earth did I get here?

One woman in particular caught my eye. Her caring husband, who practically held her up each morning, always escorted her. The pain and agony on this woman's face was very apparent. Every night when I was at home, going about life with my husband and daughters, I would find myself thinking about this particular woman. After weeks of just thinking about her, I finally listened to God. I knew He wanted me to do something.

I decided I would make dinner for her family. For some reason, I was hesitant to talk with her. Her obvious agony and pain made me feel like I didn't want to interfere. So two days before my final treatment, I went to the nurse and asked how I could go about giving this woman a meal.

With tears in her eyes, the nurse said, "Well, I have never had anyone ask me this before. This woman has six little children, and I know she would love dinner."

So I buzzed home and made a grand meal for this family of eight. I sat in bed that night picturing what I would say to her, how I would introduce myself.

In the morning, I entered the waiting room with bags full of food and a note saying that I had been praying for her and her family. When I realized the woman wasn't around, I left my gifts for her. I never found out the woman's name and, to this day, I still don't know how she is doing. But that doesn't matter. I had listened to God.

So my challenge to you is, "Are you listening?" It doesn't have to take an illness or some kind of tragedy for you to stop and just listen. All around us, men and women need an extra hug, dinner, prayer or encouragement. Take time out of your busy schedule to ask God how you can do His work. He will show you the way.

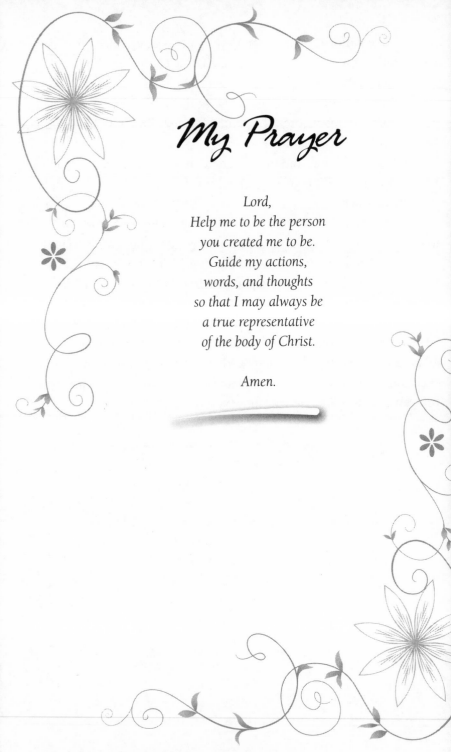

My Prayer

Lord,
Help me to be the person
you created me to be.
Guide my actions,
words, and thoughts
so that I may always be
a true representative
of the body of Christ.

Amen.

His Name Is Gary

By Karen Talcott

Blessed is he who is kind to the needy.
~Proverbs 14:21

His name is Gary. I finally found that out after months of giving him money, food, and a warm blanket. Gary is a homeless man who lives in my neighborhood. He has a shopping cart filled with his earthly possessions that I see on the edge of the park each day. Rain or shine, Gary sits in this park alone. I used to just walk up and hand money to Gary, and he would look up at me with hollow, empty eyes. I always smiled and said, "God bless you," but then walked away.

As time progressed, however, I felt more compelled to act. On the spur of the moment, my daughter and I bought a new fleece blanket to keep him warm. Much to our amazement, the temperature dropped that night, and I knew Gary was wrapped in our blanket. But this one act of compassion still made me feel empty inside. I knew that I needed to do more.

One night, I made beef stew for the family. It was hot and filling to our stomachs. As we were cleaning up the dishes, I knew that I needed to bring some of this warm food to Gary. I quickly heaped stew on a paper plate, and added some rolls and a cup of applesauce.

Then I drove to the park where Gary lived. He looked up in surprise as I walked over to him with the plate of food. At that moment, my purpose became clear. I was to bring food to Gary on a routine basis and be more than a passing acquaintance.

I am now marking my one-year anniversary of bringing food to Gary each week. Sometimes, my children come along and play in the park as I talk to him. Sometimes, I go alone.

One time, I found that Gary's fingers were covered with second-degree burns. He had used a lighter to check his clock in the middle of the night, and a small fire started. He put it out, but not before he had burned his fingers. At home, I called a friend who was a nurse and asked her how I should help him. She gave me the medical advice I needed, and I went back to the park with antibiotic cream, gauze, bandages, and medical tape. For the next week or so, I checked on him daily to make sure his fingers were not becoming infected.

At times, I wonder if Gary thinks I badger him, but I feel the need to care for him. Gary is now a real person to me, not just a homeless man. I feel blessed that God has used me in service to see beyond the human shell to the real man inside.

My Prayer

Heavenly Father,
help me to always see
the true soul that lies in the heart of all people.
Regardless of how they appear,
guide me to seek out the needy,
homeless or abused,
and realize their true identity.

Amen.

faithful friends

By Susan M. Heim

If one falls down,
his friend can help him up.
But pity the man who falls
and has no one to help him up.
~Ecclesiastes 4:10

W hen my friend, Dawn, lost her twenty-one-year-old son, Jason, in an Air Force helicopter crash in Afghanistan, her husband (her son's stepfather) and her daughters were very supportive, but they were going through their own grieving process. It was Dawn's female friends who really got her through that horrendous first year.

Her local friends called all of her out-of-state friends to break the sad news. They made sure that Dawn ate and slept and continued to care for herself. They looked after her teenage daughters, cooked numerous dinners for the family, and cleaned the house. Even after the funeral services, they continued to be there for Dawn in whatever way possible. Dawn doesn't think she would have survived her grief that first year without her friends.

And today, many years later, Dawn's friends are still coming through for her. Dawn established a scholarship fund in her son's name for students at his former high school. His passions were swimming and art, so every year Dawn and her friends hold a beautiful banquet to honor Jason and award scholarships to deserving swimmers and artists. Again, Dawn knows that she could never put this event together alone. Each year without fail, her friends are there to help with mailing invitations, lining up speakers, assessing applications, fundraising, and more.

Faithful friends make the good times better and the bad times more bearable. They are representatives of God's love and compassion during our earthly lives. Lean on your friends during times of trouble and let them bless you with their time and their love.

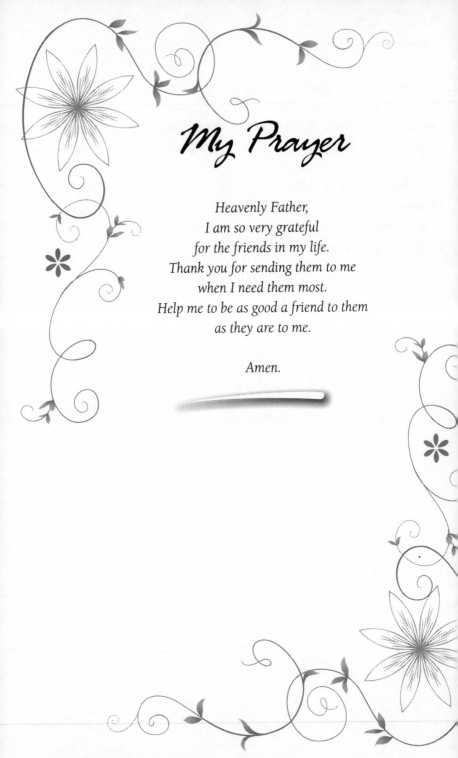

My Prayer

Heavenly Father,
I am so very grateful
for the friends in my life.
Thank you for sending them to me
when I need them most.
Help me to be as good a friend to them
as they are to me.

Amen.

A Little Girl's Prayer

By Lorie Bibbee

My sheep listen to my voice;
I know them,
and they follow me.
~John 10:27

*D*oughnuts? Really, Lord? Doughnuts?

As I walked through the grocery store, it seemed as though doughnuts were everywhere! The bakery had them on sale; the boxed ones were on the end caps; and the little white sugary ones just kept popping up in front of me! When I first noticed them, I was happy because I really didn't want them. (That was a dieting first!) But after seeing them an unusual number of times, I started praying for self-control. The funny thing was that I hadn't been tempted. At all. I simply noticed they were popping up in front of me again and again. But why? So I faced them and started praying even more earnestly. (I probably looked pretty funny facing off with the doughnuts!)

"Doughnuts? Really, Lord? Is this from you? Do you want me to buy doughnuts? I don't want them in the house. My husband doesn't want them in the house... so why doughnuts?"

I was completely clueless. But I sensed that I was simply to pick them up and put them in my cart. So I did.

"Seriously, God, the other ones, too?" I asked as I spied more doughnuts.

And then it was milk... and cheese sticks and bread and peanut butter. That was the list; it just wasn't *my* list!

After my shopping trip, I showed up at my neighbor's house. She was going through some tough financial times, and one of her six daughters answered the door. I asked if someone had prayed for doughnuts, and she started crying. They knew some even harder times were coming, and they'd been wondering if God could still hear their prayers. So one little girl prayed for God to deliver doughnuts if He still cared for them. He delivered not just one kind, but two.

My Prayer

Dear compassionate Father,
thank you so much for caring for us,
for being there for us in tough times
and in times of abundance.
We are so grateful to you
for hearing us, and for speaking to us, too.
Help us to hear your voice and heed your call...
even when you call us to buy doughnuts!

Amen.

"You're right! I did pray for doughnuts! Did you bring the pony I prayed for, too?"

80

The Server Is Served

By Jeanie McGuire Tennant

*"The King will reply,
'I tell you the truth,
whatever you did
for one of the least of these brothers of mine,
you did for me.'"
~Matthew 25:40*

I minister to a lovely ninety-six-year-old widow who has lost most of her ability to communicate due to a recent stroke. She used to be a musician, so I have found that the best way to communicate with her is through the singing of hymns and children's Bible songs. She cannot speak the words, but she hums along in perfect pitch and rhythm.

Of course, I do not know what message God is sending to her, but her eyes sparkle and she smiles. However, I am very clear about what He is doing for me. The words of the hymns actually speak to me like I had never heard the words before, and I am awakened and inspired by the voice of God. I go to serve the widow, but God uses the time to teach me, and open my eyes and heart to the love of Jesus.

I feel that I have been blessed with a calling to serve elderly widows. God has given me a patient ear for listening to the stories they often tell more than once. When I visit them, I am able to bring laughter to their lives as I encourage them to remember people and events from when they were younger, and to bring comfort when we read the Word of the Lord and pray together.

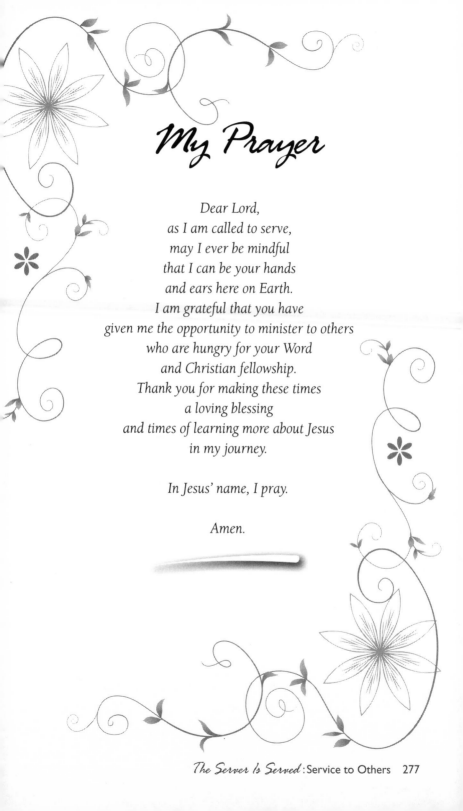

My Prayer

Dear Lord,
as I am called to serve,
may I ever be mindful
that I can be your hands
and ears here on Earth.
I am grateful that you have
given me the opportunity to minister to others
who are hungry for your Word
and Christian fellowship.
Thank you for making these times
a loving blessing
and times of learning more about Jesus
in my journey.

In Jesus' name, I pray.

Amen.

81

A Shift in Focus

By Kim Leonard

But when you give to the needy,
do not let your left hand know what your right hand is doing,
so that your giving may be in secret.
Then your Father,
who sees what is done in secret,
will reward you.
~Matthew 6:3-4

I am a breast cancer survivor, and my husband Brad and I were in Houston for some annual tests. We went to a cute little village to waste some time between appointments. Brad and I sat on a bench, and I quickly noticed a man on the bench across from us. By his appearance, I soon gathered that he was homeless. He also seemed to be mentally ill as he was having a conversation with himself.

I leaned over to my husband and said, "Please ask this man if we could buy him lunch."

I could tell Brad was a little hesitant to approach the man, who was filthy, and had huge holes in his jeans and sores on his lips. Nonetheless, Brad went up and asked him, "Can I buy you a sandwich?"

The man answered, "Yeah, yeah," so Brad went into the sandwich shop while I stayed outside.

I tried to put himself in this man's place. Young moms walked by with their children. Other people were talking on their cell phones, holding bags full of purchased items. No one paid any attention to this man.

After a bit, Brad came out with a full meal, which we handed to the man. Then I said to Brad, "Ask him what size pants he wears."

Brad looked surprised, but quickly realized where I was going with this. We buzzed to the Gap to buy an outfit.

When we showed the man the things we had bought for him, he looked into our eyes and said, "Oh, yeah? For me? Great, thank you."

Then he reached out and shook Brad's hand. Their eyes met, and there was so much love in that moment that you could feel the connection between them. Later, as Brad and I sat in our car, I saw that my husband was crying.

I realized that the Lord had sent the homeless man on the bench. Focused on someone else, thinking about another's situation, I quickly forgot about my own worries. As I waited to get the results of my MRI, the Lord taught me how powerful it is to focus on other things. When you are in a time full of worries and anxiety, ask the Lord to give you something else to think about. Maybe, just maybe, He has someone in mind for you.

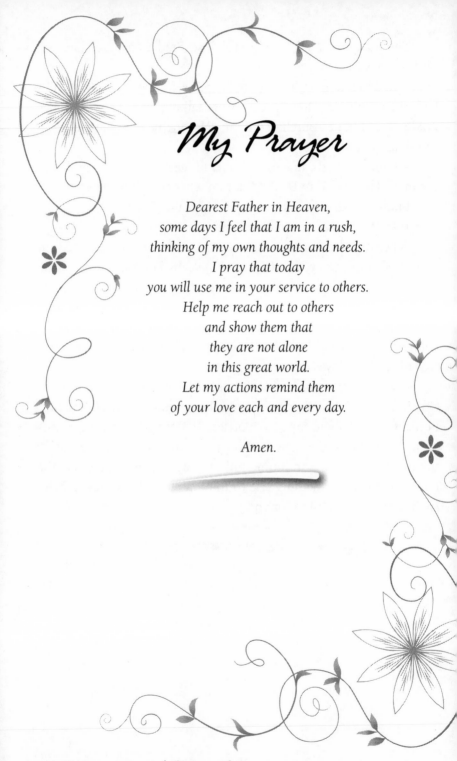

My Prayer

Dearest Father in Heaven,
some days I feel that I am in a rush,
thinking of my own thoughts and needs.
I pray that today
you will use me in your service to others.
Help me reach out to others
and show them that
they are not alone
in this great world.
Let my actions remind them
of your love each and every day.

Amen.

82

Chicken Soup for the **Soul**

More Than a Cup of Sugar

By Darleen M. Gilbert

Help carry one another's burdens,
and in this you will obey the law of Christ.
~Galatians 6:2

Sixteen years ago, my husband was diagnosed with severe heart problems after suffering a heart attack. His energy waned more each month as we kept cardiologist appointments in hopes of improving his heart health and stamina. My husband became unable to do lawn maintenance, so it fell to me to keep our large yard looking well-kept.

One Saturday morning, our neighbor showed up unannounced. When I heard his lawnmower start up near our front door, it was music to my ears! Our young neighbor realized it was too much for me to do the weekly mowing chore along with my caretaking role.

Today, thirteen years after my husband's death, Darrell is still faithfully mowing my lawn each week. He won't let me pay him, so I have given up asking and just accept his generous gift. At the end of the season, I always give him some goodies from my kitchen as a small payment for his summer-long thoughtfulness. He makes me feel less like the helpless widow next door and more like the senior lady who occasionally also needs his muscle to open a pesky jar of tightly sealed pickles.

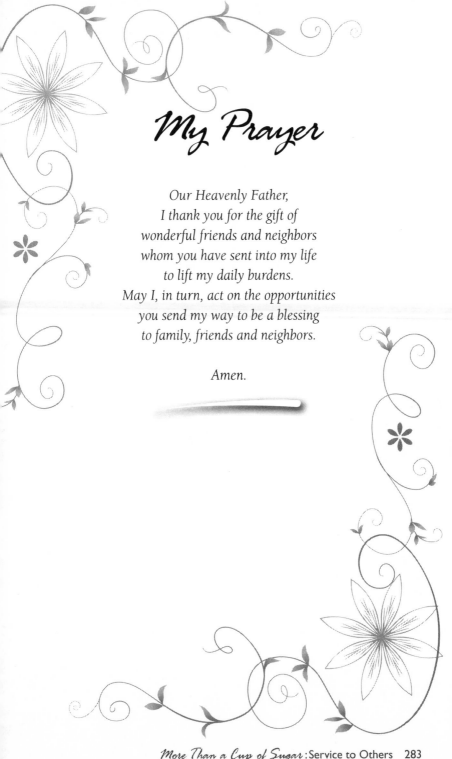

My Prayer

Our Heavenly Father,
I thank you for the gift of
wonderful friends and neighbors
whom you have sent into my life
to lift my daily burdens.
May I, in turn, act on the opportunities
you send my way to be a blessing
to family, friends and neighbors.

Amen.

83

Where Can You Make a Difference?

By Susan M. Heim

You have been a refuge for the poor,
a refuge for the needy in his distress,
a shelter from the storm
and a shade from the heat.
~Isaiah 25:4

My kids came home from school with a flyer in their backpacks. A collection was being taken for the poor. Children were asked to bring in nonperishable food, gently used clothing, household goods, and cash donations.

As I looked through our kitchen cupboards and rifled through my kids' dresser drawers, I realized how fortunate we are. The pantry was well-stocked, and I knew we wouldn't even miss the cans and boxes of food we donated. Similarly, the twins' drawers were filled with T-shirts and shorts that they had hardly worn. I felt so very blessed... but guilty.

There are so many people in the world who were born into poverty and oppression. Many don't have the opportunity or the right to receive an education, to marry who they want, to earn money, to speak their opinion. And, of course, food and clothing are often luxury items.

I know that I'm truly fortunate to have been born into a country and a family where these difficulties are rare. But I also realize that this gives me the opportunity to make a difference for others in need.

There are a million small—yet important—things we can all do to make a difference. Some people use their money to help support overseas projects. Others knit sweaters or sew clothing to send to those who can't afford them. Still others donate books so schoolchildren in other countries can learn to read. God knows the best way for each of us to reach out to others, and I trust that He will guide me on how to make a difference in His perfect time.

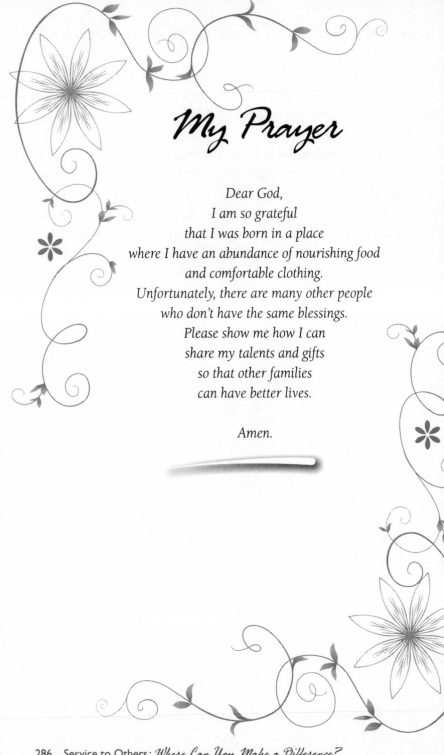

My Prayer

Dear God,
I am so grateful
that I was born in a place
where I have an abundance of nourishing food
and comfortable clothing.
Unfortunately, there are many other people
who don't have the same blessings.
Please show me how I can
share my talents and gifts
so that other families
can have better lives.

Amen.

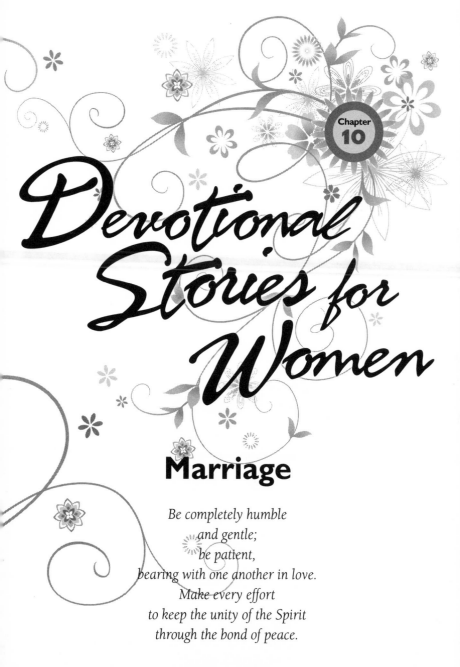

Devotional Stories for Women

Marriage

*Be completely humble
and gentle;
be patient,
bearing with one another in love.
Make every effort
to keep the unity of the Spirit
through the bond of peace.*

~Ephesians 4:2-3

84

The Authentic Spark

By Karen Talcott

However, each one of you also must love his wife
as he loves himself,
and the wife must respect her husband.
~Ephesians 5:33

*L*eland and I married a little later in life. We were both in our thirties and had a strong sense of who we were. As a newly married couple, we were able to focus just on ourselves. We took vacations, slept in most weekends, and went out to leisurely dinners. We even laughed at our friends with young children who had to eat dinner by 5:30 P.M. We were happy, but a bit self-centered.

But, as the years passed, we eventually evolved as a couple. We certainly had some difficult years in our marriage. As the children arrived, the throes of babyhood took a toll on us, and we were often short-tempered with each another. We had our fights, but soon made up. We were lucky that, as the children grew up, so did we.

These days, we still don't get out as much as we should. Romantic dinners are few and far between, but we do connect once a week at church. Sitting with my husband at church keeps my spark alive. We hold hands during the service, take time to rub each other's shoulders, and hear God's message together.

We are holy and spiritually united for this one hour a week. God provides us with the only authentic spark through the Holy Spirit. And it is up to us as a couple to let it evolve into our married life.

My Prayer

Please bring the Holy Spirit
into my life this day, dear Lord.
Help my husband and me
to renew our spark
and show our love to one another.
Be with us during the times of struggle
and guide us back to a place of peace.

Amen.

85

Chicken Soup for the Soul

Fighting Words

By Susan M. Heim

Don't have anything to do with foolish and stupid arguments,
because you know they produce quarrels.
~2 Timothy 2:23

There they were again. My husband's dirty clothes were on the floor, right next to the hamper! Would it have killed him to lift the lid and put the clothes inside? I fumed at this lack of regard for our home's appearance—and for my feelings. I'd asked him nicely in the past to pick up his clothes. I'd teased him that he would make a lousy basketball player. I'd even gotten angry and come just short of calling him a "slob."

But for my husband and me, such name-calling usually just opens up a can of worms. If I criticize his clothes on the floor, he points out all the papers scattered on my desk. So, I remind him that his workbench is a mess, and he says I never clean the crumbs from the counter after preparing sandwiches. Seemingly little issues can blow up into a major ordeal. Therefore, that day I closed my mouth and opened the hamper myself.

I know that my husband and I are not unique when it comes to fighting. Oddly enough, I sometimes wonder if even Mary and

Joseph ever fought with each other! I picture them on the long and tiring trip to Bethlehem while Mary was pregnant with Jesus.

After an arduous day of traveling, seemingly in circles, Mary might have said to Joseph, "Why don't you ask that man over there on the camel if we're on the right path to Bethlehem?"

Being a typical man and not wanting to ask for directions, Joseph may have mumbled, "I know where I'm going. You're just crabby because your hormones are raging."

To which Mary would have snapped back, "Well, you'd be grumpy, too, if you were nine months pregnant and riding a donkey all day!"

I guess if Mary and Joseph's marriage could survive the trials they faced in their lives (and certainly their problems were far worse than mine), then perhaps my husband and I have a chance as well. When my feelings escalate to the point of wondering why I ever got married, I know it's time to ask God for help. Sometimes He shows me how to resolve the issue. But other times, there is no easy answer to our disagreement. I realize then that God wants me to swallow my pride, forgive my husband and move on. It's not easy to take that first step toward reconciliation, but it's possible with God's help.

My Prayer

Dear Lord,
please help my spouse and I
to work out our differences,
to communicate better,
and to grow in love
and respect for each other
as we solve our problems.
May we see each other
as perfectly created by you—
flaws and all.

Amen.

"If you can't find Bethlehem... Could you AT LEAST try and find the nearest Oasis with a restroom?"

Closing a Door, Opening Another

By Tamilyn Sosa

And we know that in all things
God works for the good of those who love him,
who have been called according to his purpose.
~Romans 8:28

After seventeen years together, my husband said those words no wife ever wants to hear: "I want a divorce. I've found someone else."

In court, my husband was granted the divorce he so desperately wanted. It was then that I received a profound sign from God. I left the court crying and got in the elevator to scurry to my car.

The elevator operator asked me what floor I would like to go to, and then he said, "Don't worry, dear. Whenever God shuts one door, He opens another."

I looked at the man, startled, for he had no idea why I was crying, yet he had felt compelled to say that to me! The elevator doors soon opened for me to exit, as if God was saying to me, "Here's to the beginning of our new life together—you and me."

From that day on, the events that have occurred in my life are nothing short of a miracle from God. Shortly after my divorce, I inherited some money that I had no idea I was entitled to. I was able to buy a beautiful townhouse to live in. God then placed a wonderful man in my life who had experienced a very similar past and a painful divorce.

Our love story is inexplicable, as neither one of us has ever experienced the euphoria we've found in each other. Of course, it was Christ-ordained, and He's always been the center of our relationship. We were married on August 28, 1999. God gave us that wedding date for it happens to be taken from one of our favorite Bible verses: Romans 8:28.

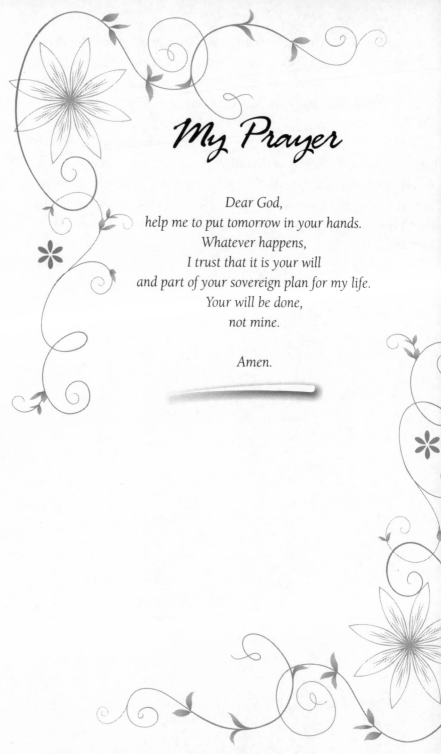

My Prayer

Dear God,
help me to put tomorrow in your hands.
Whatever happens,
I trust that it is your will
and part of your sovereign plan for my life.
Your will be done,
not mine.

Amen.

87

Prayers for a Husband

By Kathleen Johnson

Every good and perfect gift is from above.
~James 1:17

I was twenty-four. I had just graduated from law school, gotten my first job as a lawyer, and was a Sunday school teacher. On New Year's Eve, I made a deal with God. My two New Year's resolutions were to not date unbelievers and to pray for one hour daily for a husband. In return, I asked God to give me a husband by March first. I believed that husbands came from God since "every good and perfect gift is from above"!

Each day, I got up early and prayed for my husband for one hour. In early February, I went to a party at a neighbor's apartment. Also there was a guy named Rick, who seemed to be deliberately avoiding me. When I asked Rick if there was a problem, he said that there certainly was—he could not get past the idea that a person could be both a lawyer and a Sunday school teacher! I immediately explained myself and my beliefs, and we talked seriously throughout the party. When I went home that night, I tried to have no feelings for Rick because he was not a Christian.

On Tuesday evening, as I was leaving my apartment to attend Bible study, I ran into Rick. He asked if he could go with me to Bible study, and I was thrilled. Later that night, Rick invited me to a play on Thursday and to Disney World on Saturday. I agreed to go both places if he attended church with me on Sunday.

On Sunday morning, Rick loved meeting my Sunday school class of third-grade girls. That evening at church, to my shock, Rick accepted Christ as his Savior. When we left church and got into Rick's car, he told me that his new life had just begun—and he wanted me to marry him!

There are facts and there are feelings, and accepting Rick's proposal of marriage, after knowing him only eight days, was a fact—he was God's "good and perfect gift." I had none of the normal doubts of whether he was "the one" or whether I should find out more about him. Rick was God's gift to me—the one I had been praying for on my knees for the past two months.

That next Tuesday night at Bible study, my friends, who knew about my two-month prayer vigil for a husband, were incredulous when I introduced my new fiancé and showed off my engagement ring (his grandmother's). Rick and I were married four months later on June 22, 1974.

My Prayer

Thank you, God,
for hearing our prayers
and changing the physical world
with your answers.
Help us to bring every care,
concern, and fear before you
so that your will can be done in our lives.

Amen.

My Dear Lou

By Hulda Currie

For love is as strong as death...
many waters cannot quench love;
rivers cannot wash it away.
~Song of Songs 7:6-7

I met Lou Currie when I was in high school. I had decided to join the First Aid Corps as a sophomore. In the club, I met another wonderful man named Bill. He and I started dating, and we eventually married.

We enjoyed our life together and had three beautiful children. Everything in my life was going according to plan, but one day my life shattered apart. My dear Bill died quite suddenly, leaving me to raise our three children alone. I was terrified and didn't know which way to turn.

But with God's wonderful help, another plan was in motion. Lou contacted me again after his wife died. We continued our friendship, and then one night he proposed to me over dinner. My answer was a resounding "Yes!"

Lou and I celebrated thirty wonderful years together before his death. We were always close, and our life was full of love for each other. Every day, I still miss my Lou, and I look into the sky, hoping to catch a glimpse of him as clouds float by.

God had a wonderful hand in my life, and I trust that He will lovingly protect me in my remaining years. I was given the greatest gift of finding and experiencing love, not once, but twice in this lifetime. Thank you, Lord, for giving me the privilege of sharing thirty years with my dear Lou.

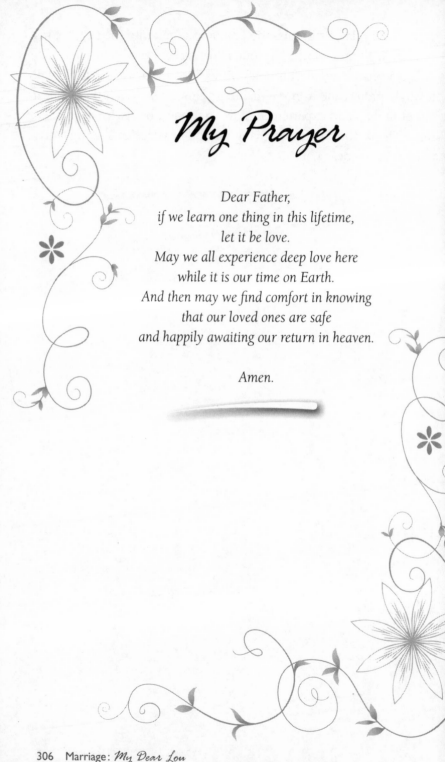

My Prayer

Dear Father,
if we learn one thing in this lifetime,
let it be love.
May we all experience deep love here
while it is our time on Earth.
And then may we find comfort in knowing
that our loved ones are safe
and happily awaiting our return in heaven.

Amen.

89

The Miracle of Acceptance

By K.P.

Shout for joy,
O heavens; rejoice,
O earth; burst into song,
O mountains!
For the Lord comforts his people
and will have compassion
on his afflicted ones.
~Isaiah 49:13

I was almost seven months pregnant and coping with the realization that my husband had relapsed yet again in his alcoholism. This came after an extended period of sobriety, a time of joy and hope, during which I got pregnant. Unfortunately, as so often happens in addiction, the recovery was too tenuous to hold.

One July evening, I walked to a nearby church for an Al-Anon meeting. For once, I was not angry at my husband. I just felt utterly defeated by the disease. That night, I needed the comfort of the familiar Serenity Prayer: "God grant me the serenity to accept the things I cannot change, the courage to change the things I can, and the wisdom to know the difference." I also yearned for the company of others who understood, as perhaps few others can.

This particular meeting was uneventful, actually quite ordinary. I sat there, I confess, mostly lost in my own thoughts. And then it happened: an awareness, I suppose. A warm light flowed completely into my mind and my heart. And with the light came a quiet voice: "You have no control over his drinking." It was not a thought. I now believed and accepted this truth.

I had hoped and prayed for the miracle of acceptance over many years. It set me free. As I walked home, I marveled at how calm and peaceful I felt. I held love in my heart for my husband, seeing his pain and struggle. I also felt clear about my reality. The time for wishing was over. I was going to be raising my child alone, whether I stayed married or not. My husband, so disabled by drinking, would not be able to fully participate as a parent.

I was no longer afraid by that thought, though. I knew, without any doubt, that God and I would walk on this journey together. He would be there to help me make the difficult decisions that needed to be made. And, when it was over, I would walk away with strength I never knew existed inside me.

My Prayer

God,
during those times
when we are at our lowest,
you somehow find a way to reach down to us.
You whisper the very words
we so desperately need to hear.
Thank you for your enduring love
in all the seasons of our lives.

Amen.

90

Chicken Soup
for the *Soul*

A Mixed Marriage

By Deborah R. Albeck

And if a woman has a husband who is not a believer
and he is willing to live with her,
she must not divorce him.
For the unbelieving husband has been sanctified through his wife,
and the unbelieving wife has been sanctified through her believing husband.
Otherwise your children would be unclean,
but as it is, they are holy.
~1 Corinthians 7:13-14

t's early December, and my husband, Bob, is in our family room performing his annual job—stringing the lights on our Christmas tree. Once he finishes, the kids and I will take over and decorate with bulbs and tinsel. I guess that's pretty typical for most homes across America. What's not as typical is that, while he is stringing Christmas lights, I am setting up the Menorah and hanging up Hanukah decorations.

"Honey, do you want me to put on one of the Christmas CDs?" Bob asks from behind the tree.

"That would be great! Thanks, honey!" I reply.

He happily pops in a Carpenters' Christmas CD and turns it up. He knows most of the lyrics to the songs.

Yes, my Jewish husband is very supportive in most every way of my religious beliefs. I attend church, Bible studies, and other events regularly. I give of my time and our finances. I prepare Easter and Christmas dinners. I pray openly. He accepts all of this out of love and respect for me, and after twenty-two years of marriage, I love him deeply. Anyone looking at us would say that being from different religious backgrounds has caused no obvious problems in our marriage. And they would be *almost* 100% right in saying so.

With all of that said, privately, I do experience some emptiness in my life because of our different religions. For all of his allowances, Bob has no personal relationship with God, just conventional Jewish traditions. I attend church regularly by myself. I pray by myself. And, most troublesome, I believe by myself.

Truth is, I pray often for patience and endurance, to keep on going by myself, hoping that one day God will provide my husband with an opportunity to desire a deeper understanding and relationship with Him. But I also know that God already has a plan for me, my husband and our children, and He will implement this plan in His own time. My job is just to keep doing what I'm doing—praying for and loving my wonderful Jewish husband.

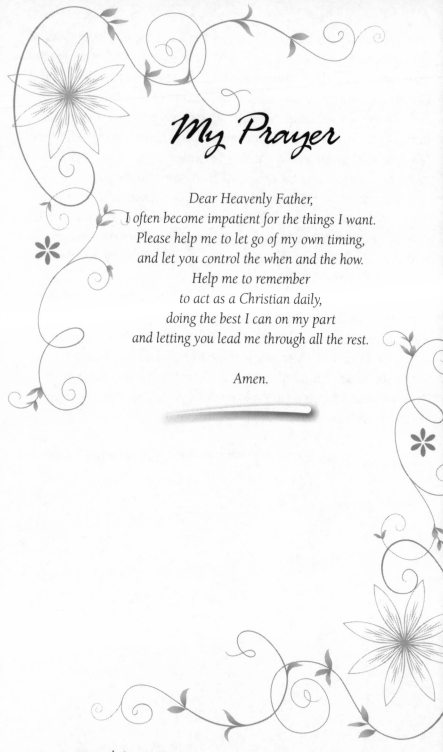

My Prayer

Dear Heavenly Father,
I often become impatient for the things I want.
Please help me to let go of my own timing,
and let you control the when and the how.
Help me to remember
to act as a Christian daily,
doing the best I can on my part
and letting you lead me through all the rest.

Amen.

91

A Cord Not Broken

By Toni Thompson

Though one may be overpowered,
two can defend themselves.
A cord of three strands is not quickly broken.
~Ecclesiastes 4:12

My husband and I have been married for more than twenty-seven years, and during that time we have realized the truth of Ecclesiastes 4:12. On our twenty-fifth wedding anniversary, we bought each other new rings with three bands entwined. The two outer bands symbolize the two of us and our love, while the center band represents God, who is at the center of our love.

In a Bible study I was in years ago, marriage was described to me as a triangle with God at the top, and the husband and wife at the bottom points, equally distant from God at the top. As the husband and wife grow closer to God, they also grow closer to each other. This is what has happened with Al and me, even though it has not always been easy or smooth.

Thankfully, our God is a God of relationships. Al and I found out very early in our lives what a "broken relationship" was. We were both divorced before our marriage to each other, but God took those broken relationships—our two halves, as Al and I joke—and made a whole family unit.

But the past five years have been very difficult for our family. At the peak of his career, my husband lost his job, and we still have not been able to recover financially. We are blessed with three daughters. One got married, and the other two have gone off to college. We wonder each month how we will get by, but God still has a precious plan for us.

We may have to work longer than we anticipated, but we know that the more love we give to each other and those around us, God blesses it and gives it back to us. We have also realized what we really need to get by—only our Lord and Savior Jesus Christ and each other. God took our two lives, added Himself, and we have become "a cord... not quickly broken."

My Prayer

Dear Heavenly Father,
thank you for my spouse
and for the love we share.
Let us continue to love you
and keep you at the head of our marriage
so we may continue to grow in our relationship
with each other and,
most of all, with you.

In the Holy name of Jesus, I pray.

Amen.

92

Chicken Soup
for the Soul

Gifts from the Heart

By Susan M. Heim

There are different kinds of gifts, but the same Spirit.
~1 Corinthians 12

The box was big. What could it be? A beautiful sculpture for the yard? A piece of jewelry disguised in an oversized box? Some imported leather luggage? I slowly opened the package in anticipation. I wanted to savor every moment before the big surprise. I peeled down one side of the wrapping and read a word on the side of the box: Hoover. Hmmm. Okay, I thought to myself, maybe the outside of the box doesn't accurately reflect the contents inside. I popped open the top of the box and pulled out my very own... vacuum cleaner! Yes, it really was a Hoover, after all. Funny, I didn't remember that being on my wish list!

"I know our vacuum hasn't been working very well, so I figured you could use this," my husband noted.

He was right. We really did need a new vacuum cleaner. But I couldn't help thinking, "Couldn't he have gotten me something more thoughtful? More personal? Why couldn't he get me a gift from the heart? Doesn't he love me anymore?"

But the more I thought about it later, the more I realized that my husband gives me gifts from the heart every day. He makes me homemade chicken soup when I'm feeling under the weather. He gets up with our twins on Saturday mornings so I can sleep in a little longer. And what woman can resist a man who does the "yucky" chores around the house, like emptying the litter box and unclogging the bathroom sink? The gifts from my husband may be much more subtle these days, but they show his love for me much more clearly than sparkly baubles in my jewelry box.

My Prayer

God,
help me to recognize
the real gifts of love that my spouse gives me.
May we continue to think of new
and wonderful ways to please each other,
not by purchasing expensive things,
but by giving more true "gifts from the heart."

Amen.

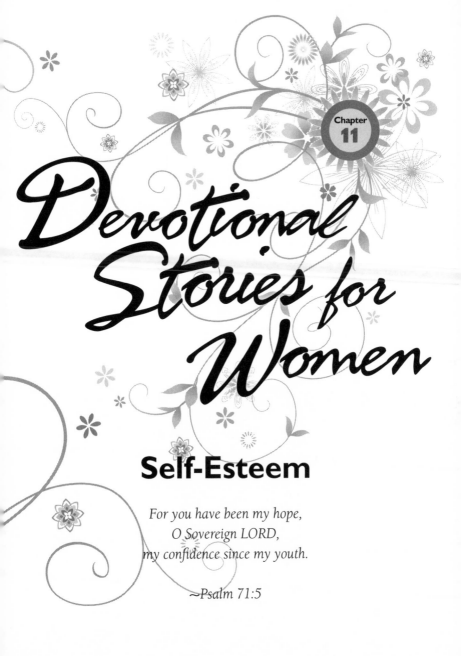

Devotional Stories for Women

Self-Esteem

*For you have been my hope,
O Sovereign LORD,
my confidence since my youth.*

~Psalm 71:5

93

Healing the Hole in My Heart

By AmondaRose Igoe

Then your light will break forth like the dawn,
and your healing will quickly appear.
~Isaiah 58:8

Every time I looked in the mirror, I found numerous reasons to dislike my body. I thought I was fat, ugly, unwanted and imperfect. I was certain that if I changed the outer me, everything in my life would be wonderful.

I started on a simple, balanced diet, which eventually turned into a vicious cycle of yo-yo dieting. Every time I gained weight or over-ate, I would beat myself up emotionally. I thought I was mentally weak for being out of control with food. Whenever I went on a diet, I became even more obsessed with my weight. I spiraled out of control.

After many years of truly irrational behavior with food, I realized that food wasn't the source of my problems. I had a deep hole inside of my heart that I was trying fill with food. I had been using food as a way to mask my insecurities.

I knew deep in my heart that only God could set me free from my food issues and heal the hole in my heart, and my prayers have been answered. It wasn't something that happened overnight—I had to be willing to grow and let go of self-defeating behaviors that no longer served me—but with ongoing prayer and a willingness to change, I can now say that I love me exactly as I am because I know God loves me. The hate and condemnation I felt toward myself are gone, now replaced with love and respect. As a result, I have a normal relationship with food and my body. The hole in my heart has been replaced with God's overflowing love.

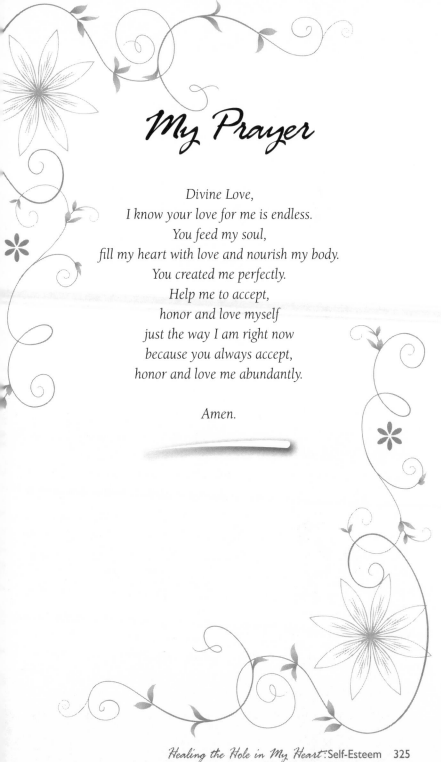

My Prayer

Divine Love,
I know your love for me is endless.
You feed my soul,
fill my heart with love and nourish my body.
You created me perfectly.
Help me to accept,
honor and love myself
just the way I am right now
because you always accept,
honor and love me abundantly.

Amen.

94

Gossip Hurts

By Karen Talcott

Though you probe my heart and examine me at night,
though you test me, you will find nothing,
I have resolved that my mouth will not sin.
~Psalm 17:3

Recently, I accepted an invitation to lunch with a group of friends. After the usual greetings and placing our orders, we got down to business. And when I say "business," I really mean "gossip." We shared about our own lives, and then started in on the other friends who were not there. We talked about one friend's divorce and all the dirty details we had heard collectively. How much money was she getting? Did he really cheat on her or was it the other way around? All of it was really none of our business, but our tongues wagged for a couple of hours.

As I drove home, I started to feel the twinges of guilt set in. Had I really said all those mean-spirited things at the table? I certainly had been active in the discussions, so I couldn't say that I was an innocent bystander. And the more I thought of my behavior, the more I wanted to hang my head in shame.

I try so hard to remain a Godly person who follows the teachings of Jesus. But in situations like these, an insecure person takes my place. It would be easy to cast a soft paintbrush to the whole picture and say that no harm comes from discreet gossip. But, in my heart, I know the truth. When we put down another person, the impact is felt, regardless of whether they hear it or not.

Why do I let my insecurities take me down this path? The real reason is that gossip takes the spotlight off of my life. By talking about someone else, it makes my troubles seem less enormous.

I hope that as I mature as a Christian, I will find the strength to exclude myself from gossip. The best course of action would be to remove myself from these gatherings where I know that mean-spirited talk will be the highlight. Jesus set the standard for unconditional love. By walking with Him on a daily basis, I know that someday I will find the power to withhold my judgment from others.

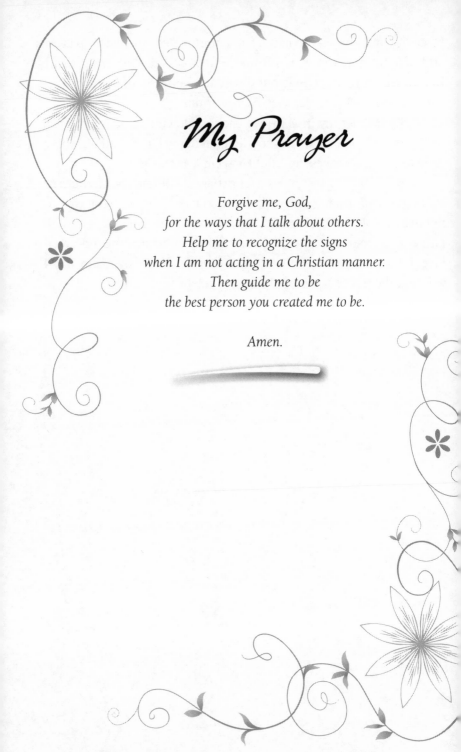

My Prayer

Forgive me, God,
for the ways that I talk about others.
Help me to recognize the signs
when I am not acting in a Christian manner.
Then guide me to be
the best person you created me to be.

Amen.

95

Chicken Soup
for the Soul

Healing the Trinity — Mind, Body and Soul

By Loretta D. Schoen

"In your anger do not sin":
Do not let the sun go down while you are still angry.
~Ephesians 4:26

had been sporting what Christian author Patsy Clairmont coins as a 'tude (attitude). I was persnickety, critical, quick-tempered, and controlling. I did not fully understand why I was this way until I had overcome several family crises, and began to fall apart physically and emotionally.

I went to a counselor with the complaint, "I cry all the time!" The counselor explained that crying was a symptom of a greater problem. The mind, body and soul are the "trinity" of the human body. If the mind and soul don't get an attitude adjustment, it can lead to physical ailments.

I began to explore myself and learned that I had been shaped by being a victim of incest. It took me a while to accept that even the good things in my life were the result of what I had survived as a child. It took even longer to be able to forgive my abuser. As long as I kept harboring that anger, the more I felt I was punishing him. Unfortunately, while I had him in my mental jail, I was imprisoned as well. I had to forgive my abuser to resolve the self-destruction in my life.

Slowly, with the help of my faith in the Holy Trinity (Father, Son and Holy Spirit), I began to heal my earthly trinity (mind, body and soul). Through daily prayer, God helped me to release my anger and pain. I began to see my abuser as a mortal man with a mental illness. Despite what had happened, I was resilient, stronger, and more able to do the work God asked me to do. I had suffered abuse, but I survived! I was no longer the victim.

God has provided me with opportunities to share my story to help others. Good has come out of my experiences, and I have grown to like the person I am, battle scars and all. Taking time with the Holy Trinity provides me with a daily attitude adjustment!

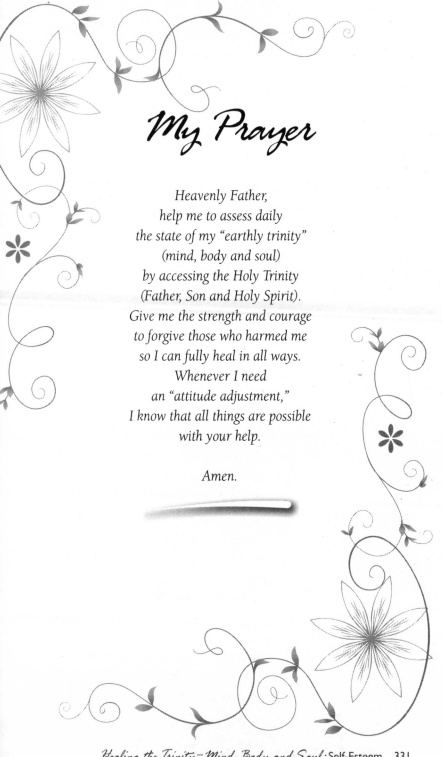

My Prayer

Heavenly Father,
help me to assess daily
the state of my "earthly trinity"
(mind, body and soul)
by accessing the Holy Trinity
(Father, Son and Holy Spirit).
Give me the strength and courage
to forgive those who harmed me
so I can fully heal in all ways.
Whenever I need
an "attitude adjustment,"
I know that all things are possible
with your help.

Amen.

96

He Holds My Hand

By LaTonya Branham

For I am the LORD, your God,
who takes hold of your right hand and says to you,
Do not fear; I will help you.
~Isaiah 41:13

Going back to school—after I had stepped out for several years—was both a scary and long-awaited dream. Marriage, a new job, children, and relocation were my excuses for the pause in my pursuit of higher education. I would always encourage others to do well in school, but my faith was weak when it came to my own desire to finish my degree. It was easier to tell someone else to do what I wasn't willing to do myself. I was also experiencing enormous feelings of doubt. Did I have the courage and was I "smart enough" to finish my degree?

I heard about an accelerated bachelor's degree program that I could possibly complete in one year. I found myself praying about it over and over. Eventually, I signed up for it. I asked God to help me get through the program, which was fifty miles from my house. The assignments were rigorous and challenging. Often I would think, "Oh, Lord, what have I gotten myself into?" But God made a way for me—He held my hand.

I remember the program coordinator telling me that my classes would meet at a seminary because there was no more space on the main campus for new students. "A seminary," I thought. "What an interesting place to pursue a degree in management!" I had asked for God's help, and He placed me right in the midst of a holy environment. Every evening while traveling to class, I would play gospel music all the way to the seminary. It certainly made a difference by lifting my spirit along the way.

After one year, I received my bachelor's degree. I pressed on and completed the requirements for a master's degree. Although I changed jobs soon after completing my degree, I realized that this time allowed me to shape my thoughts, lean on God, and move forward. Life has never been the same. God keeps His promises—do not fear!

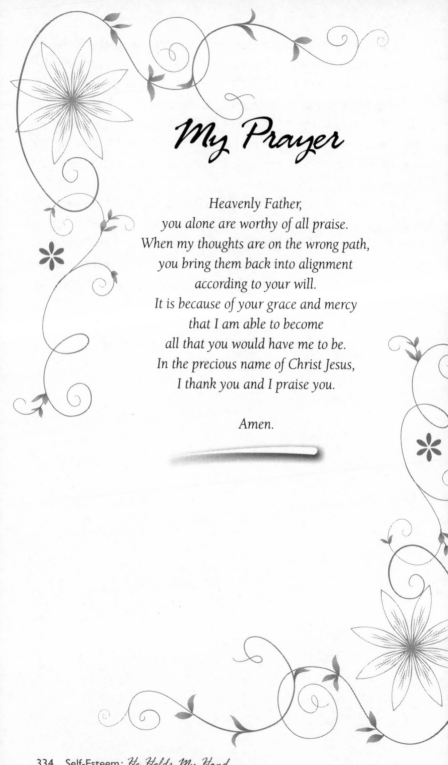

My Prayer

Heavenly Father,
you alone are worthy of all praise.
When my thoughts are on the wrong path,
you bring them back into alignment
according to your will.
It is because of your grace and mercy
that I am able to become
all that you would have me to be.
In the precious name of Christ Jesus,
I thank you and I praise you.

Amen.

97

Vanity and a Toilet Toupee!

By Loretta D. Schoen

And why do you worry about clothes?
See how the lilies of the field grow.
They do not labor or spin.
~Matthew 6:28

My mother had cancer and underwent chemotherapy, which caused her to lose all of her hair. Since my mother always hated her hair (too frizzy, too thin, and too red), we told her God was giving her a second chance, and that when it grew back in, it would be thick and straight and beautiful.

In the meantime, Mom went in search of the perfect wig. If there was a wig store within a 100-mile radius, we were there! After more than four weeks of constant shopping, she settled on a $500 wig. It was made of human hair, and had a cap like netting to help keep Mom's head cool. It was straight, thick, and a beautiful shade of auburn.

One morning, Mom used her walker to get into the bathroom. She prepared to put on her new wig by placing a stocking cap over her very bald and smooth head. She then put on the wig and adjusted it. She became frustrated because she felt that the hairs were not lying straight, and she asked if I would "fix it." I looked at the wig—a pageboy cut with bangs—and not a hair seemed out of place, which I told her.

"Can't you see that the side and back just don't seem to lay right? Here, you take the pick and fix it," Mom said.

Rather than argue, I thought it easier to take the pick and go through the motions of combing her wig straight. Unfortunately, the pick caught the wig's netting just right, and the wig flew off my mother's smooth head, leaving the stocking cap in place. The two of us watched in horror as it flew through the air, seemingly in slow motion, heading right for the toilet bowl! With both hands on her walker, my mother kept exclaiming, "Oh, my! Oh, my!"

All the while, I kept thinking, "Where are we going to get the money to replace this $500 rat... I mean, wig?!"

Mom was between me and the bowl, and there was nothing we could do but watch as the wig hit the toilet seat, teetered for a moment, and then fell... onto the tile floor! We both looked into the mirror at each other and burst out laughing. We realized that physical beauty is fleeting, but seeing the humor in life is a gift from God.

My Prayer

Abba Father,
help us to remember
that our heart and soul need care,
for they are what make us beautiful!
When our outer appearance
becomes a source of strife,
may we recall that we are all beautiful in your sight.
Physical beauty may be temporary,
but the beauty within us will never die.

Amen.

"You look great, Mom... but it's your inner beauty I hope I inherit!"

98

Chicken Soup for the *Soul*

Just as I Am

By Adleen Rawlings

*Blessed is the man
who does not condemn himself.*
~Romans 14:22

I was born in the Deep South in a small town in northern Georgia. When I was nearly ten years old, my family moved to Michigan. Going from the quiet South where everyone knew your name to a strange land where nothing was familiar was like moving to another country! Because I was "different," I was often teased and made fun of, and as a result I developed a huge inferiority complex that lasted most of my life. I was shy and felt no one liked me.

I got married right out of high school and started a family soon afterward. I was blessed with three beautiful daughters with whom I kind of grew up.

God was always in my life, but I slowly moved away from Him and into myself. Slowly, I was led to a 12-Step Program because of an addiction in my family, and through this program my relationship with God was revived. I started attending and becoming involved in church again.

What I've learned through all of my experiences is that God loves me just as I am. He made me a unique being, and there's no one like me. God knows every hair on my head. Not everyone will like me, but that's okay with me now. I finally like myself, and I know I am special and loved.

My Prayer

Dear Father,
thank you for always being with me
every step of the way,
and for giving me the wisdom
to rise above the trials of life.
Thank you for building me up
when I was down,
and letting me know
that I am special and loved.
I pray that all of your children
feel beautiful and unique in your sight.

Amen.

99

Money Well Spent

By Karen Talcott

I know what it is to be in need,
and I know what it is to have plenty.
I have learned the secret of being content
in any and every situation,
whether well fed or hungry,
whether living in plenty or want.
~Philippians 4:12

The time had come for my husband and me to have a serious talk about our finances. We had been living outside of our means and now needed to rein in our spending habits. We came up with a budget and promised to stick faithfully to it each month. But, before we left the room, my husband added this last admonishment: "Karen, this budget even includes your weekly trips to Target. You have got to start spending less."

As I began the process of tracking my expenses, it made me realize how Americans have a love of stuff. It can be brightly wrapped under a Christmas tree, come in the form of a new car, or be our "dream house." But it all boils down to the material things. How many times have I looked in my big, overstuffed closet and declared I had nothing to wear? How many hundreds of dollars have I spent on beauty products over the years? Could I really find an eye cream that would diminish the fine wrinkles around my eyes?

It seems that my dollars and cents are tied to how I feel about something when I purchase it. I feel better for that one moment when I buy it, and then those emotions evaporate into thin air. It is one big, vicious cycle that repeats itself with a consistency for our entire lifetime. But is there more to life than this?

Of course there is, and our faith in God well the proof. So why do we listen to one message on Sunday and practice a completely different one the remaining six days of the week? Think back to a sermon about tithing and giving 10 percent of our income to God. Did you see people squirm in their seats? I know that I did because I was one of them.

What would I hear if I spent more quiet time with God each day? I know it would be a message about doing *more* and spending less. Do more for those less fortunate, those feeling alone, and those around the world who barely survive. Spend your time and energy abundantly, but save the money for the necessities and charities close to your heart. God's priority has always been His beloved people. It is this message I hope we remember when times are rough.

My Prayer

Dearest Father,
I have a need to fill up my life
and home with things.
I pray that with guidance from you,
I can begin to set new priorities.
Help me to see the people
and situations around me
that really deserve my money.
Show me ways to grow
as a person and Christian
with each expense that I make.

Amen.

My Fading Looks

By Susan M. Heim

Charm is deceptive,
and beauty is fleeting;
but a woman who fears the Lord
is to be praised.
~Proverbs 31:30

Many years ago, my father was walking down a city street on his way to pick up my mother at her office. He saw a woman ahead of him who was speaking vivaciously to another person. He was fascinated by how alive and vibrant she looked, and he stopped and said to himself, "What a strikingly beautiful woman."

After a moment, he continued on his way, but as he got closer to this woman on the street, he made a surprising discovery. The woman he had been captivated by was his wife — my mother — more lovely than ever to him after more than twenty years of marriage.

The older I get, the more I fret about my own ability to elicit that "Wow!" look from my husband that my mom still gets from my dad. Glancing through old photo albums can be a sobering experience. The beautiful hair I see in those old pictures is now flecked with gray (at least until I make it to my hair colorist), and wrinkles are taking over my once-smooth skin. Looking at the beautiful air-brushed and surgically enhanced movie stars in magazines makes a further dent in my self-esteem. I am no longer the young woman that my husband married.

But, deep down inside, I know that our relationship is based on more than an admiration of each other's looks. We're raising four wonderful children; we've built a home together; we share our faith in God; and, we have a history together that nobody else has experienced.

When my husband looks at me now, his eyes of love don't see the new wrinkles or gray hairs. They still see the same girl he married many years ago. In God's eyes, we are always beautiful. Thankfully, God has bestowed this same unconditional capacity to love—and a pair of rose-colored glasses—on our loved ones.

My Prayer

God,
thank you for making us "perfect"
in your likeness.
May we always see the same beauty
in each other that you see in us.
Please help my spouse to continue
to see me with the same loving eyes
that he had when we first married.

Amen.

I Am Worthy of Love

By Sharlene H. McClendon

I praise you because I am fearfully and wonderfully made.
~Psalm 139:14

Five years ago, I found myself lost and alone, wondering what I was supposed to do with the life I had chosen but could no longer understand. I had moved into my third home — bigger and better than the last one, according to the world's standards — but I was more miserable than ever.

After moving into our home in May, my husband got hurt on the job, and I found myself pregnant with our third daughter. In a two-year span, I gave birth to two daughters, while my husband remained unemployed. At the same time, I was struggling to find out who I was and what I was destined for. There were times when I wanted to walk away from everything and everyone connected to the life I had chosen.

I started attending a church that offered small groups. After taking a class called Making Peace with Your Past, the door was opened to better understanding myself. I had spent so much of my life giving to others because I was scared to receive love in return. In this class, I learned that it's okay to give *and* receive love.

I walked out of this class with the freedom to experience all of God's gifts—love, hugs, smiles and peace. I now look at life in a whole new way. I share and show His love to all with whom I come in contact, whether I know them or not.

If you are feeling lost and alone in the life you chose, like I was, remember that by accepting and loving yourself, you open yourself up to God's greatest gift—His eternal love for you.

My Prayer

Dear Lord,
when I am tempted to
feel undeserving of love,
I remind myself
that you have made me in your image.
I am "wonderfully made"!
I am so grateful
to be worthy of your love,
and to be able to
share the good news of your love
with those I meet.

Amen.

Devotional Stories for Women

More Devotion
Two Extra Stories by Jennifer Sands

Meet Our Contributors
Meet Our Authors
Thank You
About Chicken Soup

A Rose, a Vase, a Ring and a Cross

By Jennifer Sands

For where your treasure is,
there your heart will be also.
~Matthew 6:21

My husband, Jim, was killed in the attack on the World Trade Center on September 11, 2001. I was not a believer in Christ before then; God used that tragedy to bring me close to Him and to introduce me to the saving love of Jesus.

I still wear my engagement and wedding rings, and that has proven to be confusing for some people. Either they assume I've remarried, or they find it odd that I would continue to wear them as a widow. When they ask me about it, I tell them that the rings still symbolize the love that Jim and I had for each other, but now they have an additional meaning: they represent the commitment I have made to Jesus, and the unending love He has for me. Some people are satisfied with that answer. Some people get teary-eyed and say, "Oh, that's *sooo* beautiful..." Others just walk away perplexed, scratching their heads.

Another piece of jewelry that I wear every day is my cross necklace, and there's a story behind it. In my first book, *A Tempered Faith*, I described myself as a single, red rose and Jim as an expensive vase. One day, the vase came crashing to the ground and left the rose all by herself. She was alone—devastated, lost, thirsty, and dying. As the rose, I had a choice: either shrivel up and become a stick of thorns or look for water so I would live and never thirst again. Jesus offered me living water (John 4:14). I immersed myself and found new life in Him.

After my best friend Amy read my book, she was deeply touched by that chapter and gave me the most beautiful cross necklace I've ever seen. It has a silver rosebud in the center of the cross and its stems and leaves extend out to form the beams. And Amy's words to me were the best part of the gift: "Now the rose isn't dying by itself anymore. Now the rose is alive, *with* the cross."

She summed up my whole testimony with one piece of jewelry and one profound statement. And since the same people who ask about my wedding ring usually ask about my necklace, too, I get to share this story with them. The cross necklace is not just material treasure made of sterling silver, it's also spiritual treasure because it's a great witnessing tool for the love of Christ. Jesus, who wore a crown of thorns for me, went to Calvary so that I could one day be an eternal rose with Him.

My Prayer

Dearest Lord Jesus,
when the jewelry box
of my heart is wide open,
I see You...
the authentic, precious cornerstone
who shines above all else.
Thank You for Your endless love,
Your abounding grace,
and Your manifold wisdom.

Amen.

Standing on the Promises of God

By Jennifer Sands

Blessed is the man who perseveres under trial,
because when he has stood the test,
he will receive the crown of life
that God has promised to those who love Him.
~James 1:12

A few years ago, I had the old gray carpet in the living/dining area of my house torn up and hardwood floors put down. Before the new wooden planks were installed, I invited my family and church friends to come over and write their favorite Bible verse on the sub-flooring with a thick, black, permanent marker. The floor was covered with Scripture from one end of the room to the other, along with their names and the date they wrote their verse. Some of them got creative. In the area where the piano would be placed, my brother wrote Ephesians 5:19-20: "Sing and make music in your heart to the Lord, always giving thanks to God..." Under the dining room table, my brother-in-law wrote John 6:35: "Jesus said, 'I am the bread of life. He who comes to me will not hunger and he who believes in me will never thirst.'" My own contribution was Jeremiah 29:11, my life verse: "For I know the plans I have for you," says the Lord. "Plans... to give you hope and a future." The hardwood floors were eventually laid on top of our Bible verses and now, as we walk around that room, we can say that we're "standing on the promises of God."

Hardwood floors are strong, sturdy, resilient, and they don't wear out quickly. In the material world, we usually pay more for such items because they last longer and are therefore more valuable. With respect to durability, you usually get what you pay for.

I'm not very useful to the Lord if I tire out quickly. Believe me, there were many times in the past eight years when I was close to throwing in the towel: After my husband was killed on September 11. After his underwater Memorial was destroyed by a Category 5 hurricane. After I was diagnosed with breast cancer. But God gave me all the grace I needed to persevere through those struggles. Like hardwood floors, my value is partially determined by how well I hold up when people or things walk all over me. The more durable I am, the more valuable I am to God... and fortunately, He gives me the strength I need to become durable!

With respect to durability, we usually get what we pay for. Yet amazingly, we can get eternal life even though we didn't pay for it. By God's grace through faith in His Son, *we* get what *Jesus* paid for, and that will last forever.

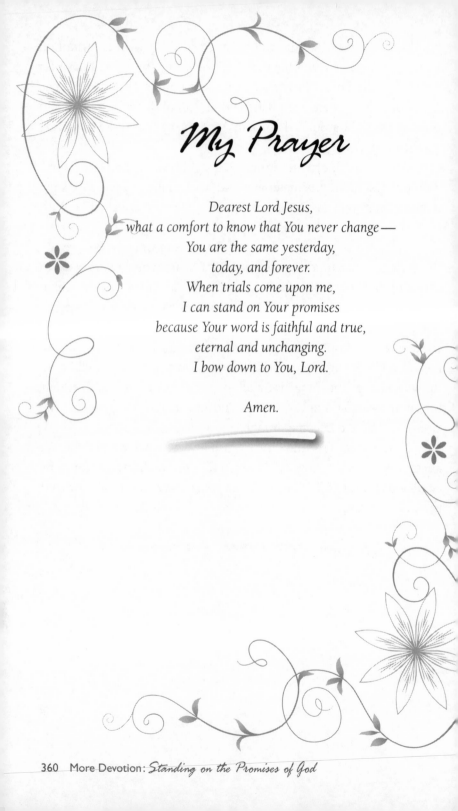

My Prayer

Dearest Lord Jesus,
what a comfort to know that You never change—
You are the same yesterday,
today, and forever.
When trials come upon me,
I can stand on Your promises
because Your word is faithful and true,
eternal and unchanging.
I bow down to You, Lord.

Amen.

Meet Our Contributors

Debbie Albeck and her husband, Bob, live in South Florida while her two children attend college. Although her background is in health care, Debbie actively volunteers at nearby schools, her church, and community. She plans to become involved with environmental protection issues. E-mail Debbie at Debbie.Albeck@gmail.com.

Catherine Berg received a BS from the University of Central Oklahoma and an MA from the University of Texas at Dallas. She has been published in *Sojourn Journal*, *Taj Mahal Review*, *Virginia Woolf Miscellany*, *Mad Hatters' Review*, and *Dallas Arts Review*. Contact her via e-mail at bergblane@aol.com.

Lorie Bibbee lives with her husband and four children. She loves storytelling, writing, and speaking to ladies when she and her family aren't traveling to new places and trying new things. She plans to continue writing and speaking to teenage and adult women. Please e-mail her at Lorie.Bibbee@yahoo.com.

Olivia Bibbee is an exciting young author. She has recently had poems published in two books and is continuing to write at an amazing pace. She plans to write and publish short novels and other imaginative stories.

Janis Bonnie is a proud wife and mother of two wonderful children. She works for the family business, Joe Bonnie & Son Moving, and is a distributor for Juice Plus+. She enjoys spending time with her family. Please visit her websites at www.janisbonniejuiceplus.com and www.joebonniemovers.com.

LaTonya Branham earned an MA from Antioch University McGregor, and a BS from Wilberforce University. She is a college administrator and an adjunct professor. LaTonya and her husband live in Dayton, Ohio, and devote their time to youth and community outreach ministries.

Cathy Carpinello is happily married and the mother of three teen-age children. Her passion is reaching students with the love of Jesus Christ. She coaches cheerleading, supervises the middle school praise and worship band, and serves as "lunch lady" at her children's school. E-mail her at Kahoca@aol.com.

Julie Cruz received her BA from Florida International University in 1991. She is a stay-at-home mom of three. She enjoys volunteering, traveling, and attending Bible studies.

Hulda Currie notes that "to be without my wonderful Lou took the wind out of my soul. I do know he is in good hands—God's hands. Love you, Lou!"

Cindy Dumke is a small business owner in South Florida. She enjoys spending time with her family, reading, writing, boating, and enjoying nature. This is her first experience writing for publication.

Carrie Ellis received her bachelor's degree in 1983 and her Juris Doctorate in 1987. She practices law, and enjoys cooking, camping, hiking, and traveling. Carrie started writing as a teen, and enjoys writing poetry and real-life stories of inspiration. Her love of storytelling developed from her cherished grandmother, who turned real-life stories into bedtime tales. You can e-mail her at mommykitten61@yahoo.com.

Andrea Federman moved from her home in Bavaria, Germany, to South Florida in 1991. She graduated with a major in English and achieved her degree in hotel management. Andrea has a passion for editing and proofreading, as well as writing inspirational stories and poems. Please e-mail her at acoffeegirl67@hotmail.com.

Elizabeth Fenn received her BS in nursing from Purdue University in 1994. She worked as a pediatric oncology nurse for nine years before staying home with her three children. She and her husband have enjoyed watching their children grow and explore the world around them.

Susan Forma is a licensed massage therapist and Reiki master. She enjoys teaching her clients, family and friends about living a non-toxic life filled with essential oils, healthy living, and a positive attitude. She lives with her two children in South Florida. For more information, contact her at healthandharmony@bellsouth.net.

Being the sole support of her children for most of their childhood has given **Gail Frank** the inspiration to start writing. In addition to true stories of miracles, she also writes children's stories and poems. Gail hopes to compile these stories into a series of books and turn them into cartoon features from which children can learn.

Cynthia J. Freels is a retired RN. She is the mother of five and grandmother of eleven. Cynthia spent ten years working with homeless families and some of the most wonderful people you would ever want to meet. She likes to travel, read, sew, and work in her gardens.

Jacqueline M. Gaston received her BS in 1989 and MEd in 1996. She is a special education teacher in Virginia. Jackie resides with her four beautiful children and supportive husband, and aspires to become an author. Please e-mail her at jgaston5@comcast.net.

Darleen M. Gilbert is a grandmother of eight and a great-grand-mother of one. She attended Willamette University and Oregon State University. For twelve years, she has volunteered in the second-grade classroom of her daughter, a teacher. Inspired by a writing class, she has written *Stories of My Life*, a gift for her children and grandchildren.

Charlene F. Gossett holds an associate's degree in Broadcasting and Practical Theology and a bachelor's degree in General Studies. She enjoys reading, running and NASCAR. She also teaches first-graders in Sunday school. She is currently writing her first NASCAR romance novel and has plans to write inspirational books for women. Please e-mail her at shilo98@bellsouth.net.

Christina (Stina) M. Harris received her BA in Literature from Ramapo College and is a member of the National English Honor Society. A freelance writer, she plans to have her first novel published sometime this year. Please feel free to contact her via e-mail at charris110384@gmail.com.

Carol Holmes is married to Steve, and is the mother of four children and grandmother of ten. Carol likes to refer to herself as a "domestic engineer" or, in other words, a housekeeper. She loves music, singing in the church choir, and spending time with her family.

AmondaRose Igoe specializes in helping entrepreneurs and business owners communicate their message clearly, concisely, and powerfully. AmondaRose teaches her clients how to connect with the mind, heart and spirit of their audiences, which makes her a highly sought-after professional speaker, author, public speaking trainer, and coach. Contact AmondaRose at www.HighPerformanceSpeaking.com.

Kathleen Johnson has been an attorney for thirty-five years. She is a cum laude graduate from the University of Georgia and received her Juris Doctorate from the University of Florida. She is a member of Phi Beta Kappa. Kathleen and her husband have one daughter, Katy, who was Miss Vermont and Miss Vermont USA.

Deborah L. Kaufman has enjoyed working in international adoption, domestic foster care, and teaching English to middle- and high-school students. She is a wife, mother, and proud grandmother. Deborah enjoys reading to excess, teaching Bible study, and writing inspirationals and romantic suspense. You may e-mail her at dlkaufman@bellsouth.net.

Kimberly Kenney received her BA, with honors, from Purdue University in 1994. She is a homemaker and is busy raising her three amazing boys. Kimberly enjoys exercise, volunteering, and spending time with friends and family.

Nancy Kershaw is an Oregon State University extension faculty member. She lives in Netarts, Oregon, and works with the 4-H program. Nancy enjoys spending time with her family, traveling, reading, and walking the family dog on the beach.

Gerri Kinley resides with her husband and three children. She received her BA in education from Florida Atlantic University, and has taught and tutored elementary school students. Gerri has also distinguished herself as a professional mezzo soprano soloist in South Florida.

Francinne Cascio Lawrence, MRE, MSW, is author of the *Baby on Your Hip* gift-book series and a mother of three. A popular keynote speaker, she enjoys sharing the message that parents deserve to be as hip and happy as their baby. Please e-mail her at francinne@babyonyourhip.com.

At age thirty-three, **Kim Leonard** was diagnosed with breast cancer. She spends her time reaching out to others who are suffering with the disease. Kim and her husband Brad have three girls. She enjoys spending time with family and friends. She also enjoys running and Pilates. Contact Kim via e-mail at kleonard@indy.rr.com.

Sharlene H. McClendon has been married for seventeen years and has four girls. She is currently taking classes in psychology at Liberty University. Sharlene loves leading and attending small groups. In addition, she enjoys traveling, reading, and writing. She plans to write inspirational materials to help women accept and love themselves. Please e-mail her at sharlene_mcclendon@att.net.

Laura Bartolini Mendelsohn is a spiritual counselor who helps people heal and live their dreams by accessing the wisdom and guidance of Spirit. Using spiritual tools in her own life, Laura has achieved spinal healing, straight As in school, financial independence, and a first marriage after age forty-five. Contact Laura through her website at www.lauramendelsohn.com.

God went from **Lisa Murphy's** head to her heart several years ago. She now feels like she's in love every day. Lisa's favorite Christian quote is "I can't answer all the questions, but I can't deny the experience." Lisa prays that you experience God's love and purpose in your life.

Janice Flood Nichols earned her BA from Seton Hill College and MEd from the University of Pittsburgh. As the author of *Twin Voices: A Memoir of Polio, the Forgotten Killer*, she devotes her time to speaking about the importance of polio eradication. Visit her website at www.twinvoices.com.

Mary O'Reilly-Seim is an Angel Therapy Practitioner® certified by Dr. Doreen Virtue. She writes and publishes inspirational messages for spiritual growth. Her Words of the Ages daily messages, inspirational calendars, and posters are available at www.yourabundantlife.net.

Maria Rodgers O'Rourke is a popular and accomplished speaker, columnist, and teacher. Author of the *Prepare Your Heart* series of devotional journals, she inspires and guides others to recognize and embrace the hidden meaning in life. Maria and her husband have two children. Visit Maria at www.MariaRodgersORourke.com.

K.P. lives and works as an educator on the west coast with her now ten-year-old child, her husband, and a motley assortment of pets. She enjoys writing, teaching, and all outdoor activities. Her current goal, to master Sudoku, is progressing slowly and painfully.

L.P. is devoted to her family and believes firmly in guardian angels.

Stephanie Piro lives in New Hampshire with her husband and three cats. She is one of King Features' "Six Chix" (she is the Saturday chick!). Her single panel, "Fair Game," appears in newspapers and on her website: www.stephaniepiro.com. She is also an illustrator, a designer of gift items for her company Strip T's, and a part-time librarian. Contact her at stephaniepiro@gmail.com.

Tracy Powell currently resides in Arizona with her family. She embraces adventure and enjoys writing, horses, scuba diving, and traveling. Feel free to e-mail her at thenickeringnag@yahoo.com.

Nancy Purcell teaches creative writing in the adult education program at Brevard College and coaches new writers. Nancy is retired, and loves gardening and travel. She recently completed her first novel.

Adleen Rawlings is a retired co-owner and general manager for the business she and her husband owned and sold in 2002. She now loves spending time with grandchildren, traveling, walking, singing in church choir, golfing, and volunteering at her church. Please e-mail her at rawlingsad@aol.com.

Melody Riccardo is a mother of six children and a grandmother to three. She is still surfing, and loves nature, animals, and the arts. Melody dreams of inspiring others through lessons learned in life.

Melody is currently creating art molds and castings with her husband/sculptor, Chris. Contact them at chris@ChrisRiccardo.com or Casecolt@aol.com.

Sandra Brese Rice, married to Jeffrey and mother of Zachary and Emma, was a Lutheran school teacher for thirteen years. She then became a Parish Ministry Consultant for Bethesda Lutheran Communities where she still visits schools to do disability awareness presentations. Sandra enjoys singing in the worship band at her church.

Clara Riveros was born in Colombia, South America. She has three daughters and lives with her youngest, Melissa, who has Down's syndrome. Clara retired and enjoys spending time with her six grandchildren, but she spends most of it with Melissa's busy training schedule for Special Olympics.

Phyllis Saxton's love of words is one of the greatest gifts her mother ever gave her. Some of the most important gifts can't be held with your hands, but only felt with your heart! This is Phyllis's first attempt, at age seventy-seven, at having her writing published.

Loretta D. Schoen grew up in San Paolo, Brazil, and Rome, Italy, and now resides in Florida with her husband, two cats, and two dogs. She enjoys traveling, working with abused animals, and spending time with her grandson, Aiden. She is currently writing medical stories to inspire and empower patients.

Christy Holstead Semple is a writer and speaker about positive living. She and her husband teach these practices through their firm, The Kind Deeds Company. The birth of their daughter has inspired Christy to write an inspirational children's book about love. Please e-mail her at chsemple@comcast.net.

Holly Shapiro-Robillard is happy in her new position as CEO of the household after working twenty-two years in the title insurance industry. Holly enjoys both indoor and outdoor activities that include her family. She also enjoys reading, cooking, and walks on the beach. Please e-mail her at hashap@bellsouth.net.

Ingrid Michele Smith was born in Jamaica, and has lived in Miami, Florida, for the past thirty-eight years. Since her husband's passing in 2004, she has grown spiritually and developed an interest in the angelic realm. Ingrid loves to travel and is the proud mother of two sons, Michael and Steven.

Robin Smith thanks God. She comes from a wonderful family and has an amazing husband, Steve. They have four incredible children: Mikayla Joy, Caleb, Stephen, and Emily. She has a BA from Messiah College and enjoys teaching kindergarten. She loves motherhood, basketball, the beach, and fishing.

Tamilyn Sosa has been an insurance agent since 1987. She enjoys reading, writing, and praying. Please e-mail her at tamijose @bellsouth.net.

Jennifer Stango received her BS in nursing from the Indiana University of Pennsylvania in 1992 and practiced as a critical care nurse until she became a stay-at-home mom with her four children. She enjoys running, volunteering at her church, and spending time with her family.

Sandra Diane Stout received her associate's degree in Business Studies from Indiana University Kokomo and is a graduate of the Institute of Children's Literature. She is a Recording Secretary at Indiana University. Diane enjoys directing church drama and designing costumes, and is an accomplished pianist. She writes children's non-fiction. Please e-mail her at dstout@iuk.edu.

Jeanie McGuire Tennant is a Christian wife and mother, and a leader in her church. She has worked as a teacher, director of technology transfer for two universities, director of an innovation and entrepreneurship institute, and president and CEO of a technology business incubator. She has bachelor's and master's degrees in education.

Toni Thompson and her husband, Al, have been married twenty-eight years and have three grown children and two grandchildren. She enjoys leading Bible studies, crocheting, and making jewelry. She also writes for church publications. She started writing to pass along life stories and prayers for her children.

Audrey Valeriani is an author, columnist, self-esteem and relationship coach, board chair of Self Esteem Boston, and founder of The R.E.A.L. Women's Club. Her book, *Boot Camp for the Broken-Hearted: How to Survive (and Be Happy) in the Jungle of Love*, was a finalist in the National Best Book Awards 2008. Visit her website at www.bootcampforthebrokenhearted.com; e-mail her at theaccidentalexpert@comcast.net.

Meet Our Authors

Susan M. Heim is a longstanding author and editor, specializing in parenting, multiples, women's and Christian issues. After the birth of her fraternal twin boys, Austen and Caleb, Susan left her desk job as a Senior Editor at a publishing company and has never looked back. Being a work-at-home mother allows her to follow her two greatest passions: parenting and writing.

Susan's books include *Chicken Soup for the Soul: All in the Family*; *Chicken Soup for the Soul: Twins and More*; *Boosting Your Baby's Brain Power*; *It's Twins! Parent-to-Parent Advice from Infancy Through Adolescence*; *Oh, Baby! 7 Ways a Baby Will Change Your Life the First Year*; *Moms of Multiples' Devotions to Go*; and, *Twice the Love: Stories of Inspiration for Families with Twins, Multiples and Singletons*. Susan also hopes to venture into fiction writing in the future.

Her articles and stories have appeared in many books, websites, and magazines, including *TWINS Magazine* and *Angels on Earth*. Susan writes an online column for *Mommies Magazine* called "Loving and Living with Twins and Multiples." She shares her thoughts and experiences about raising children in today's world through her blog, "Susan Heim on Parenting," at http://susanheim.blogspot.com. Susan is also an expert on twins and multiples for AllExperts.com, and a parenting expert for SelfGrowth.com.

Susan is the founder of TwinsTalk, a website where parents share tips, advice and stories about raising twins and multiples, at www.twinstalk.com. She is a member of the National Association of Women Writers and the Southeastern Writers Association.

Susan is married to Mike, whose ever-present support enables Susan to pursue a career she loves. They are the parents of four active sons, who are in elementary school, high school and college! You can reach Susan at susan@susanheim.com and visit her website at www.susanheim.com. Join her on Twitter and Facebook by searching for ParentingAuthor.

*K*aren Talcott is an accomplished author of books dealing with women's, multiples and Christian issues. She is also a sought-after speaker/lecturer on a variety of Christian and religious topics.

The past few years have been exceptionally busy for her. In addition to *Chicken Soup for the Soul: Devotional Stories for Women*, her book, *Moms of Multiples' Devotions to Go* will be published in fall 2009. Her work was also included in *Chicken Soup for the Soul: Twins and More*. She has a variety of new projects in the works, including several children's books, another twins book, and many more devotional short stories. One day, she hopes to have enough time to finish the novel that has long been simmering.

Karen's experience in writing came from fifteen years in the classroom and a master's degree in curriculum from Oregon State University. In addition to teaching classes in grades 3-6, Karen was instrumental in setting school curriculum at the school district in which she taught. While no longer teaching elementary school, Karen continues to share her experiences and knowledge through her writings and speaking engagements. She is also a member of the Society of Children's Book Writers and Illustrators.

After the birth of her twins and caring for a toddler daughter, Karen decided to focus her attention on freelance writing. Her husband, Leland, and three children, Kara, Griffin, and Taylor, are very supportive of her writing, for which she is thankful.

Born in the beautiful state of Oregon, Karen now resides in Florida. She finds her best inspiration comes in the morning on her long walks with her two golden retrievers. Story ideas and titles seem to flow as she communes in God's world. In her precious spare time, she enjoys her children and their many sports and activities, gardening, walking, faithfully attending her local church, and watching movies with her husband.

*J*ennifer Sands' life drastically changed on September 11 when her husband was killed in the World Trade Center attacks. She was not a believer in Christ before then; God used that tragedy to bring forth her spiritual transformation and a writing and speaking ministry. God continued His work through her when her life changed again in 2007 as she was diagnosed with breast cancer. In her latest book, *A Treasured Faith*, Jennifer candidly shares her heart and her struggles with treatments. But *A Treasured Faith* goes far beyond a battle with cancer: it is the treasure that results from our joys and our trials. It is the wealth discovered when we dig deeply into the Bible and into our soul. It confirms the truth that the most valuable riches are obtained through a close relationship with Jesus Christ.

Jennifer's first book, *A Tempered Faith*, details her emotional and spiritual journey in the first year after the terrorist attacks. In her second book, *A Teachable Faith*, she passes on the lessons and Biblical truths that God has taught her. Her third book, *A Treasured Faith*, completes the "ATF Trilogy." Readers will be astounded at the rapid progression of Jennifer's spiritual growth and Biblical understanding since 9/11.

Jennifer has gained a reputation as one of today's most dynamic Christian authors and speakers. Every audience can identify with her powerful, universal message of overcoming trials through faith and trust in God. She has received extensive media coverage including featured appearances on *The 700 Club*, *Hour of Power*, Moody Bible Radio, *Homelife* magazine cover story, *USA Today* cover story, and many other broadcast and print media.

For more information, visit www.jennifersands.com.

Thank You

We appreciate all of our wonderful family members and friends, who continue to inspire and teach us on our life's journey. We have been blessed beyond measure with their constant love and support.

We owe huge thanks to all of our contributors. We know that you pour your hearts and souls into the stories that you share with us, and ultimately with each other. We appreciate your willingness to open up your lives to other Chicken Soup for the Soul readers. We can only publish a small percentage of the stories that are submitted, but we read every single one, and even the ones that do not appear in the book have an influence on us and on the final manuscript. We strongly encourage you to continue submitting to future Chicken Soup for the Soul books.

We would like to thank Amy Newmark, our Publisher, for her generous spirit, creative vision, and expert editing. We're also grateful to D'ette Corona, our Assistant Publisher, who seamlessly manages twenty to thirty projects at a time while keeping all of us focused and on schedule. And we'd like to express our gratitude to Barbara LoMonaco, Chicken Soup for the Soul's Webmaster and Editor; Chicken Soup for the Soul Editor Kristiana Glavin, for her assistance with the final manuscript and proofreading; and Leigh Holmes, who keeps our office running smoothly.

We owe a very special thanks to our Creative Director and book producer, Brian Taylor at Pneuma Books, for his brilliant vision for our covers and interiors. And none of this would be possible without the business and creative leadership of our CEO, Bill Rouhana, and our president, Bob Jacobs. Finally, we praise God for guiding us through every step of putting this book together. His presence is truly felt in every page.

Chicken Soup for the Soul
Improving Your Life Every Day

*R*eal people sharing real stories—for fifteen years. Now, Chicken Soup for the Soul has gone beyond the bookstore to become a world leader in life improvement. Through books, movies, DVDs, online resources and other partnerships, we bring hope, courage, inspiration and love to hundreds of millions of people around the world. Chicken Soup for the Soul's writers and readers belong to a one-of-a-kind global community, sharing advice, support, guidance, comfort, and knowledge.

Chicken Soup for the Soul stories have been translated into more than forty languages and can be found in more than one hundred countries. Every day, millions of people experience a Chicken Soup for the Soul story in a book, magazine, newspaper or online. As we share our life experiences through these stories, we offer hope, comfort and inspiration to one another. The stories travel from person to person, and from country to country, helping to improve lives everywhere.

Share with Us

We all have had Chicken Soup for the Soul moments in our lives. If you would like to share your story or poem with millions of people around the world, go to chickensoup.com and click on "Submit Your Story." You may be able to help another reader, and become a published author at the same time. Some of our past contributors have launched writing and speaking careers from the publication of their stories in our books!

Our submission volume has been increasing steadily—the quality and quantity of your submissions has been fabulous. Starting in 2010, we will only accept story submissions via our website. They will no longer be accepted via mail or fax.

To contact us regarding other matters, please send us an e-mail through webmaster@chickensoupforthesoul.com, or fax or write us at:

Chicken Soup for the Soul
P.O. Box 700
Cos Cob, CT 06807-0700
Fax: 203-861-7194

One more note from your friends at Chicken Soup for the Soul: Occasionally, we receive an unsolicited book manuscript from one of our readers, and we would like to respectfully inform you that we do not accept unsolicited manuscripts and we must discard the ones that appear.